D1572936

GEORG JENSEN
SILVERSMITHY
77 ARTISTS
75 YEARS

Renwick Gallery of the National Collection of Fine Arts

Smithsonian Institution Press, Washington, D.C., 1980

Published on the occasion of an
exhibition organized by and held at the
Renwick Gallery of the National
Collection of Fine Arts, Smithsonian
Institution, Washington, D.C.,
February 29 — July 6, 1980

Photographs are courtesy Georg
Jensen Sølvsmedie A/S, Copenhagen; Jan Faul, photographer,
except pages 6, 9, 11, 13, 15, and
17 (top).

ISBN 0-87474-801-1 paper
ISBN 0-87474-800-3 cloth

*Library of Congress Cataloging in
Publication Data appears on page 128.*

CONTENTS

INTRODUCTION

LLOYD E. HERMAN *Director*
Renwick Gallery of the
National Collection of Fine Arts
Smithsonian Institution
Washington, D.C.

The gleam of silver has for centuries entranced craftsman and patron alike. Revering it in their homelands, America's colonists brought silver with them to record their status in a new land, and silversmiths were soon producing new luxury goods —candlesticks, bowls, boxes—in the colonies so that these new Americans might make clear their cultural position to others.

To the eighteenth-century colonist it was important to be fashionable in clothing, silver, furniture, and other consumer goods, to keep up with the latest styles from England or France. Contemporary styles were important in ways quite different from today. In products of value (which they might expect to pass on to the next generation), Americans now often show a preference for designs recalling the past—the eighteenth and nineteenth centuries. These expensive would-be heirlooms seem safer purchases when they are in styles recalling a past heritage rather than reflecting only a current aesthetic taste.

It is not surprising, then, that in the United States companies that produce sterling silver flatware and holloware—teapots, bowls, and other serving pieces— exhibit little interest in producing and promoting styles of today. Those that do usually develop their contemporary designs in stainless steel rather than sterling silver, apparently considering that the tastes of consumers who would buy modern designs are more attuned to a material suited to less formal entertaining.

This is not to say that manufacturers and individual silversmiths in the United States have failed to produce contemporary designs of distinction in silver. Sharon Darling in *Chicago Metalsmiths* (Chicago Historical Society, 1977) documents the successes of Clara Welles's "Nordic" designs for the Kalo Shops. In existence from 1900 until 1970, this company is only one example of a small successful smithy in the twentieth century. It is important to note, however, that in their modernity the products of the Kalo Shops and other small metal companies, as well as of individual silversmiths, followed a "Scandinavian" tendency once they had advanced beyond the stylistic influence of the Arts and Crafts Movement in the 1920s and '30s. Darling concedes that the influence of Georg Jensen on American silversmiths was virtually inescapable, saying that "his work was so compelling that no modern metalsmith could ignore it."

Even today, several flatware patterns produced by American companies in either stainless steel or sterling silver attest to a persistent, if slight, interest in Nordic modern design. At the same time, others produce—in limited quantities—modern designs without obvious Scandinavian characteristics. These have been introduced at various times when a market for contemporary design has sporadically asserted itself. In creating holloware or flatware, independent silversmiths today rely almost entirely on commissions from individuals or organizations; the cost of silver does not permit many craftsmen to speculate on a market for such luxury goods. Many instead confine their production to jewelry and other more readily saleable objects.

It is the unique influence of Georg Jensen on independent silversmiths and manufacturers in the United States that prompted the Renwick Gallery of the National Collection of Fine Arts to consider producing an exhibition and book that would

Georg Jensen.

examine the continuity — and consistency — of the company's production of modern silver during the past seventy-five years. This remarkable creative output was hardly the work of one man, as many still imagine, but the perpetuation of a standard of excellence in contemporary design and technical achievement originally established by Georg Jensen's own work, then developed in new directions by seventy-six other designers who, over seventy-five years, have fostered a "Georg Jensen look." The look is not just that of the early classics created by Jensen himself or Johan Rohde with their simple columns or their draped garlands. It includes as well the rounded and geometric forms of jewelry designs from the 1950s and the somewhat more starkly modern shapes designed by Henning Koppel and Søren Georg Jensen in the 1970s. A standard of design is maintained, nevertheless, that is universal, whether in silver or pewter or stainless steel. The products made by the Georg Jensen Silversmithy from designs provided by a number of creative artists seem consistent in the way they respond to the time at which they were introduced. They were and are distinctly Modern.

GEORG JENSEN

ERIK LASSEN *Director*
Danish Museum of Decorative Art
Copenhagen

A Name

As almost everyone knows, the name Georg Jensen is that of the famous Danish silversmith. The name also stands for the world-famous firm of silversmiths in Copenhagen. The name, furthermore, identifies the group of artists and craftsmen who, throughout the years, have created silverwork from their own designs for the company. Among these artists and craftsmen Georg Jensen's name has, of course, pride of place. Since 1904, when the Georg Jensen Silversmithy was established, a number of designers and craftsmen have been associated with the firm in some form or other, their work being produced under their own names but executed at the Jensen silversmithy. This was the practice as long as Jensen lived, and since his death in 1935 new artists, designers, and craftsmen have taken their place. Altogether between seventy and eighty artists and independent craftsmen have designed and executed silverwork for Georg Jensen. Finally, it should be noted that the name Georg Jensen is associated with a style in silver. There are many facets to this style, since many artists have contributed to it. Virtually all those working in the smithy during Georg Jensen's lifetime were influenced to a greater or lesser degree by the master silversmith himself, but the most independent of these, such as Johan Rohde, preserved in their work certain of their own individual characteristics, yet always designed within the framework of a recognizable "Georg Jensen style." The style underwent many modifications in the course of approximately thirty years, from the establishment of the smithy until Georg Jensen's death—it would have been strange if this had not been so—but the basic characteristics lived on, and many of the designs of Georg Jensen and his early associates are still produced, side by side with the work of younger designers.

A notable break with Jensen's original style occurred somewhere around 1930, when Sigvard Bernadotte began to design silverwork for the Georg Jensen Silversmithy. The newly formulated Georg Jensen style continued after World War II, after artists such as Henning Koppel, Magnus Stephensen, and Søren Georg Jensen joined the silversmithy. Throughout the life of the firm, however, regardless of stylistic modifications, the name Georg Jensen has stood for silverwork expressing the spirit of the twentieth century. Georg Jensen's has never made reproductions of antiques; Georg Jensen's has always been a modern firm.

To understand the phenomenon of Georg Jensen, the man and the style, it is necessary to know more of Georg Jensen's life, of the history of the silversmithy, and the character of some of his early associates.

The Craftsman Who Wanted to Be an Artist

On the thirty-first of August 1866, the year after the close of the American Civil War, Georg Jensen was born in Raadvad, Denmark, a small industrial town in the middle of Jægersborg Deer Park, to the north of Copenhagen. Several of the original factories and houses are still there, and Raadvad's stainless steel knife blades are still mounted with Jensen silver handles, although the original steelworks at Raadvad have long been closed. Through the park ran the Mill Stream, the water of which was a prerequisite for the grindery. Georg Jensen's father was a grinder.

Georg Jensen in his workshop, 1904.

In 1926 Georg Jensen wrote a number of brief memoirs of his youth for the Danish art journal *The Collector (Samleren)* in which he recalled the woodland scenes of his happy childhood:

Raadvad was paradise on earth, the loveliest of woods with magnificent oaks and beech trees, with its large mill pond, from which the stream that drove the water mill divided itself into two arms and flowed further through the low lying meadows, with the mysterious alder thicket, where the crows gathered together in large flocks just after sunset and screamed out so that they could be heard from a great distance. . . .

Even today, in the woods around the old factory it is possible to feel something of the atmosphere that seized the young man's imagination and assuredly came to mean much for his art.

Georg Jensen started as a general hand in a Raadvad foundry and later advanced as apprentice in the braziers' workshop. He also went to school, but as a boy of the working classes school gave him little; although he read widely, he was never able to write or spell correctly. When Jensen was fourteen years old he and his family moved to a small flat in Copenhagen. His parents, having clearly seen how able he was with his hands, decided to apprentice him to a goldsmith. After only four years he was considered a qualified journeyman. The Sunday-school Movement had at the time been established for the purpose of supplementing the education of the sons of craftsmen with elementary skills, and Jensen attended one of these schools. There he had proficient teachers in drawing, geometry, and perspective and got to know the architect J. D. Herholdt, the painter Heinrich Hansen, and the sculptor Theobald Stein. Later he pursued evening classes at a technical school, taking further courses in engraving and modeling. He supported himself by working as a goldsmith during the day.

At the technical school he met Christian Joachim (who was later to become director of the porcelain factory Aluminia and the Royal Copenhagen Porcelain Manufactory), who wanted to be a painter. Georg Jensen was most determined to be a sculptor. On his way to and from the school in Ahlefeldtsgade he would wander across Ørstedspark where he would enjoy the newly erected classical bronze sculptures. He had started modeling in clay as a boy, and now he felt ready to show the sculptor Theobald Stein a bust he had made of his father.

Professor Stein did not exactly encourage Georg Jensen to study art, but he took an interest in the poor young craftsman who was so hardworking. When Jensen eventually confided to the sympathetic professor that he was preparing for the entrance examination of the Royal Danish Academy of Fine Arts (Kunstakademiet), Stein's only comment was "Really? I thought you were a goldsmith!" Nonetheless, Stein permitted Georg Jensen to model in his studio in his spare time, and it was not long before the determined student was accepted at the academy.

At the time it was unusual for a boy with a working-class background to get very far in society. The education afforded at school was poor and the curriculum extended over only a few years. But if a boy showed signs of artistic talent, the life of an artist promised him new possibilities of social advancement. In the world of art there were no class barriers.

Georg Jensen, The Harvester, *1891, bronze. Collection: Georg Jensen Sølvsmedie A/S, Copenhagen.*

Georg Jensen joined the sculpture class of the academy in 1887 — at a time when the last of the classical traditions sustained by Bertel Thorvaldsen's pupils was ebbing and a French-influenced realism was beginning to struggle with a style-conscious sculptural form that combined symbolic content and decorative effect. Jensen's few sculptures are marked by the contrasting artistic currents of his time. *The Harvester (Høstkarlen)*, 1891, is realistic, weakly recalling the work of the Belgian Constantin Meunier, whereas *Spring (Foråret)*, 1896, in the form of a young female nude, attracted a certain amount of attention through its efforts at a stylized, decorative grace. None of Jensen's sculptures evinced a particularly plastic talent, however, nor was Jensen able to sell them. Yet, upon completion of his studies at the academy in 1892, he was qualified to apply for scholarships and awards. Throughout his efforts to become a sculptor, Jensen had never ceased to earn his living as a goldsmith for he needed the income: he had married in 1891 and now had two sons.

Because he could not earn a living from his sculpture — not many in Denmark could — Jensen began making ceramics with Christian Joachim. The director of the Danish Museum of Decorative Art (Kunstindustrimuseet) helped him obtain a post as modeler at the Bing & Grøndahl Porcelain Manufactory, but it was at an unfortunate moment for a young man with his own ideas. J. G. Willumsen's obsessive preparation for the factory's participation in the International Exhibition of 1900 in Paris forced him to give preference to those artists who would work in his established way. Georg Jensen's stay with the firm was not long. The work he completed in his own workshop was more successful. A vase, *Girl with Jar (Pigen med Krukken)*, 1899, was bought by the Danish Museum of Decorative Art, and one critic wrote that it had ". . . a breath of the Greek spirit about it" — a quality one has difficulty seeing in it today.

There is no doubt that Georg Jensen's sculptures and ceramics attracted favorable attention. In 1900 he was granted the major travel award of the academy and went to Paris to expand his studies. In the meantime he had suffered a severe personal blow: after a marriage of only a few years duration, his young wife died.

During his stay in Paris he sat for the artist Ejnar Nielsen, who painted a stylized, somewhat melancholic portrait of him in profile. Jensen is shown looking at one of

Georg Jensen, Girl with Jar, *1899, ceramic. Collection: Danish Museum of Decorative Art, Copenhagen.*

Ejnar Nielsen, Portrait of Georg Jensen, *circa 1900, oil on canvas. Collection: Danish Museum of Decorative Art, Copenhagen.*

his vases. This lovely painting, rather advanced for its time, is in the possession of the Danish Museum of Decorative Art. On his return to Denmark, Jensen again took up his work with ceramics, but it did not provide him with enough money to support his family, especially since he had remarried and his second wife had presented him with a daughter. "Pressure of circumstances," wrote Jensen in his memoirs, "forces me to take up my old craft."

The Silversmith

When Jensen was almost forty years old, he faced a major turning point: he decided to become an independent silversmith and give up his long-cherished dream of being a sculptor. He never relinquished the title of sculptor, however, for the rest of his life he listed himself as *orfèvre sculpteur* in the manner of the early goldsmiths of the French court. Later when he could afford it, he had his statue *The Harvester* (see page 11) cast in bronze. It stands today in the courtyard of the silversmithy in Copenhagen, a reminder of Jensen's thwarted hopes.

Of great significance in Georg Jensen's decision to return to silversmithing was his association with the talented artist Mogens Ballin, who created highly original work in metal. Ballin is remembered today for his revitalization of pewterwork in Denmark. While working as a foreman for Ballin, Jensen met the silver designer Johan Rohde. With Ballin, Jensen created his first jewelry, which was bought by the Danish Museum of Decorative Art. This gave him the courage to establish his own workshop. A businessman lent him the money to rent a small shop, and on the nineteenth of April 1904 Jensen opened his first workshop in the courtyard of 36 Bredgade. Each morning he hung on the outside wall of his shop a display case containing his silverwork; each evening when he closed the workshop he took it down and carried it back indoors. This was the extent of his public display. In this same year, 1904, he exhibited his jewelry in the Danish Museum of Decorative Art for the first time.

The Jewelry

In his jewelry Georg Jensen created a new style that was not modeled on any style of the past. Made of silver, his jewelry was inexpensive and incorporated amber, malachite, moonstone, and opal—none of which demanded excessive investment. His jewelry was addressed to the openminded middle-class with a sense for the artistic and not to the upper-class for whom jewelry meant first and foremost precious stones in elaborate settings. Closest to Georg Jensen's work at the time was that of Thorvald Bindesbøll's. Bindesbøll, however, never used stones and his ornamentation was almost completely composed of abstract cloud motifs. In contrast, Georg Jensen never completely gave up the world of flowers and insects that he had known and loved from his childhood days in the woods and meadows around Raadvad.

Although the work of the French goldsmith René Lalique, seen by Jensen at the Paris International Exhibition of 1900, may have been a factor in prompting him to

Georg Jensen, Buckle, design introduced circa 1910, hand-chased and cut sterling silver, mounted with garnets, number 75.

resume his goldsmith work, there is no question of specific influence. A wide gulf separates the Frenchman's sophisticated, refined work and the Dane's simple, clearly designed brooches and buckles with colored stone as the dominating, sensitively placed ornament. A contemporary critic wrote of Jensen's work: "Even in the smallest button for one or two kroner, the molten silver had been granted all the fullness of form with which the metal can be imbued."

Georg Jensen's first jewelry workshop no longer exists. It was one of those low, badly lit rooms built above the arched entryway of an old Victorian townhouse of which many were to be found in the area around the Bredgade. Apart from the master goldsmith himself, the workshop included a journeyman, and soon an apprentice, Henry Pilstrup, was added to the staff. Pilstrup started at the workshop when he was fourteen years old and developed into a proficient craftsman who executed much of Jensen's jewelry. He was later to serve as foreman of the jewelry workshop. In later years Pilstrup recalled his old master:

When he arrived in the morning he pulled a pile of designs out of his pocket — they had been drawn on whatever piece of paper he could lay his hands on, sometimes he had drawn on torn-off wrapping paper. He worked quickly, in an afternoon he could fill up a sheet of sketches, all the while he sat singing his own songs to his own melodies.

The new silversmithy did not enjoy a secure financial situation. Payments had to be made on the loan Jensen had contracted to cover the cost of wages, silver, and semiprecious stones. And Georg Jensen was not a businessman. To be sure he was economical, with inexpensive personal habits, but he had to support a large family. Only a year or two after he established his workshop his second wife died. He married again and soon had three more children to support. In 1908 the workshop boasted a staff of nine but was old fashioned and without technical aids; the silver was still melted in an ordinary stove used to heat the premises. Jensen also charged too little for his jewelry, but that meant more customers — and more hard work. The workshop premises eventually were extended to take in an old half-timbered wing, which still stands today.

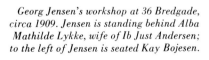
Georg Jensen's workshop at 36 Bredgade, circa 1909. Jensen is standing behind Alba Mathilde Lykke, wife of Ib Just Andersen; to the left of Jensen is seated Kay Bojesen.

Johan Rohde, Cutlery, Acorn Pattern, design introduced 1915, sterling silver with stainless steel blades, number 130.

Holloware and Flatware

Jewelry created Georg Jensen's name, but jewelry is sensitive to changes in fashion, and fashions change faster than jewelry. Jewelry is made to be worn, not to lie in the glass display cases of a museum. Yet it must be admitted that in the museum the work retains the artificial patina, the mat gray tone, and the shadows of oxidation, which Georg Jensen had learned from the Japanese by way of Johan Rohde. In the display case the fine chasework is not destroyed by wear and tear and repeated polishing. Regardless of where the jewelry may eventually be displayed, however, the designer must follow the changing taste of his clients.

So far as the customers' continued favor is concerned, holloware and flatware have a longer life than jewelry. Good models can be repeated year after year and establish a tradition of taste. One of the silversmithy's flatware designs from 1915, the Acorn pattern by Johan Rohde, is still the most sold today. Georg Jensen's first work in holloware was a small teapot with a transverse ivory handle. On the lid a flower is mounted above three leaves. The tense bright surface is rendered lively by hammer marks made while the teapot was shaped and added after the work was formed. The teapot was later supplemented by other pieces to make up a full service, and the design is still of unrivaled quality. The contrast between a living, full-bodied volume and the finely worked ornamentation showed Jensen's sensitivity to form: he was, after all, a sculptor. His contemporary critics regarded the style as a beneficial simplification—something, perhaps that might surprise a later age that has often viewed ornamentation with a critical eye. Describing the Jensen style, a French critic wrote:

Georg Jensen, Teapot, design introduced 1905, pot spun in two sterling silver pieces, cast feet individually chased, blossom decoration and ivory handle individually shaped, number 62.

The sober-mindedness of his work, which is never to be confused with poverty, has the advantage that it does not detract with useless fantasy from the fundamental qualities of the object, its proportion, its movement, and its excellent material.

In contrast to his later work from 1915, mentioned earlier, his first flatware design from 1908, the Continental pattern, is characterized by striking sobriety, very different from his numerous decorated spoons. The small elegant filings between double grooves at the base of the handle were probably inspired by a Norwegian wooden spoon. Originally the design was used on only one side; later the design appeared on both sides in answer to preferences from abroad.

A European Reputation

Georg Jensen, Cutlery, Continental Pattern, design introduced 1908, forged, hand-hammered, and polished sterling silver, number 72.

There was no want of recognition by Georg Jensen's compatriots. The Danish Museum of Decorative Art made liberal purchases of his earlier work, and his Copenhagen clientele continually grew. Nevertheless, it was abroad that Jensen gained

Der dänische Silberschmied, Georg Jensen's second shop in Berlin, on the Budapesterstrasse, circa 1926.

his fame and at times—like his great compatriot Hans Christian Andersen, also humbly born—he was more famous in other countries than in Denmark.

"The first foreigner who visited me at my workshop on the Bredgade was museum director Osthaus from Hagen in Westphalia," recalled the sixty-year-old silversmith in 1926, "and in him I found a great and faithful admirer and supporter, just as his museum was the first place abroad where my work was exhibited." This was in 1905.

Georg Jensen's work was indeed first recognized in Germany. Carl Dyhr, an alert book and antique dealer from Ålborg, Denmark, had for some time been Georg Jensen's jewelry agent. When Karl-Ernst Osthaus—soon followed by representatives from other German museums—began to make large-scale purchases, Dyhr took the risk in 1909 of opening a shop, Der dänische Silberschmied, in Berlin on the Kurfürstendam at a time when it had not yet become a prestigious shopping street. The shop was a success and until the outbreak of war in 1914 carried ninety percent of the Jensen workshop's production.

Sales went so well that there were plans for opening shops in Paris, London, and New York. The Jensen smithy in Copenhagen had become too small, in spite of an extension. The workshop was moved to more spacious premises and a sales shop was opened on the Bredgade. In 1910 Jensen was awarded a gold medal at the Brussels International Exhibition.

The outbreak of war ended the progress Georg Jensen had been making on the Continent, and all plans for the new shops had to be abandoned. In 1915 Germany prohibited the import of silver, and Jensen was forced to close his shop in Berlin. Lean times followed for the Georg Jensen Silversmithy.

The Associated Artists

Over the years, many artists have been associated with the Jensen workshops, each making his or her individual contribution. Some remained for the major portion of their careers, while some, such as Kay Bojesen, began as apprentices to the Georg Jensen Silversmithy and later made their own way.

By the beginning of World War I the artist Johan Rohde had designed silverwork for Georg Jensen for many years, even though he and Jensen entered into a formal contractual relationship only in 1917. Now there was suddenly no money available for paying him or the other artists. Their acquaintanceship began before the turn of the century when Georg Jensen showed his sculpture *Spring* at The Free Exhibition (Den Frie Udstilling), which Rohde had organized in opposition to the official exhibition held in Charlottenborg Palace. They met later at the workshop of Mogens Ballin. Rohde married in 1903 and, like other Danish artists, started to design objects for his own home—cupboards, desks, chairs, and silverware. Some of the spoons and forks were executed by Ballin. Later in 1906 Rohde designed a coffee pot with creamer and sugar bowl that Georg Jensen executed. This very beautiful unornamented work with its sophisticated unpretentiousness does not resemble either Georg Jensen's or Johan Rohde's later work.

15

Johan Rohde, Clock, design introduced 1919, bent, chased, and shaped sterling silver, number 123.

Harald Nielsen, Candlestick, design introduced 1930, hand-forged, sculpted, and chased sterling silver, number 113.

With short breaks, Rohde, who also designed silverware and various objects for a number of other Copenhagen silversmiths, began a relationship with Jensen that was to last a lifetime. Although they differed in ability, training, and temperament, Jensen and Rohde greatly respected each other. Both, in their individual ways, contributed to what the public would look upon as the Georg Jensen style, and they influenced each other. Some of the silverwork is peculiar to the one, some to the other, but there are many designs that only an expert could attribute. Particularly during the war years when their public was chiefly Danish, much of their work was overly elaborate, as judged by today's standards. This is especially true of the special orders and requests from the wealthy, whose patronage during such difficult times was not to be taken lightly. Simplicity was not seen as a virtue.

Some associates were recruited from Jensen's immediate family. His brother-in-law Gundorph Albertus was employed as a chaser after he had completed his training abroad. He also designed for the workshop and later, when he took charge of production, ensured that the high quality of craftsmanship was maintained. Another brother-in-law, Harald Nielsen, was first apprenticed as a chaser and was later employed as a designer. It has been said with justice that "much of the work that bears Georg Jensen's and Johan Rohde's names was in fact executed after rough sketches and prepared for production by Harald Nielsen." During the years between World War I and World War II Nielsen designed a considerable number of holloware articles and one or two flatware patterns. In the early years of the silversmithy, apart from the master silversmith himself and Johan Rohde, Harald Nielsen independently contributed most to the consolidation of the Georg Jensen style. After World War II he became codirector and later took over the leadership in the design and artistic side of the firm. Even though their ideas about silver might be foreign to him, he was sympathetic and responsive to young, talented designers.

Two of Georg Jensen's sons joined the smithy as designers. The second-eldest son, Jørgen Jensen, received a sound training in Germany before he started working for his father. The second-youngest son, Søren Georg Jensen, was a sculptor, and his significant silverwork had an influence on the Jensen image in the years after World War II.

To support the many artists who made their contributions as designers, the workshops were staffed with an unparalleled group of goldsmiths and silversmiths who, although they remain anonymous, must be credited with maintaining the extraordinary technical quality associated with the Jensen productions.

New Expansion, New Markets

World War I closed Western European markets and at the same time opened new ones. At the Baltic Exhibition in Malmø, Sweden, in 1914, the Swedish art dealer Niels Wendel (who later became a Jensen partner) bought everything that Georg Jensen exhibited, and in the following year at the Panama-Pacific International Exposition in San Francisco, the newspaper-king William Randolph Hearst bought the greater part of the work exhibited by Georg Jensen. Sales in Denmark increased

Frederik Lunning, who introduced Jensen silverwork to America, and an unidentified woman in the company's first shop in New York, circa 1924.

during the war, and Sweden virtually took over Germany's role as major buyer. As a result, large investments in new premises, labor, and materials were needed. To raise capital the smithy was converted into a joint-stock company. The sales operation later was organized as a separate company under the leadership of another of Georg Jensen's brothers-in-law, Thorolf Møller.

The years of expansion during World War I were followed by a difficult period; but the smithy gained a strong chairman, for both business and financial management, in P. A. Pedersen (who later became director) and an excellent sales chief in Frederik Lunning. Then in 1924 the first shop in New York was opened, and the American adventure began, initiating a new phase in the international recognition of Georg Jensen.

Innovation before and after World War II

Harald Nielsen, Serving Dish with Cover, design introduced 1930, sterling silver.

Harald Nielsen, Cutlery, Pyramid Pattern, design introduced 1927, sterling silver with stainless steel blade.

The years between the world wars saw a shift toward a more simple style in holloware and flatware, particularly in the work of Harald Nielsen. He was not uninfluenced by the new post-1920 classical taste or by the functional design much in evidence at the Stockholm Exhibition (Stockholmsudstillingen) held in 1930. Nonetheless, he continued to adhere to the tradition that considered ornament the crowning decorative touch to form. In contradistinction to Georg Jensen and Johan Rohde, however, Harald Nielsen preferred ornament that was stylized rather than natural as is clearly seen from his handles, cover knobs, and the like. His forms, moreover, are generally smooth with only one shaped profile. In 1927 Nielsen's flatware design, the Pyramid pattern, was introduced and for its time it shows remarkable simplicity. All the handles are quite smooth and end in two profiles, one smaller than the other, and a small knob.

The most decisive departure from the earlier Georg Jensen style, as has been mentioned, was made after 1930 with the work of Sigvard Bernadotte. The then twenty-three-year-old Swedish designer had artistic blood in his veins. His mother, Crown Princess Margareta, was a talented painter, and his great-uncle Eugen was called the "Painter Prince." For a short time he attended the School of Decorative Arts of the Royal Swedish Academy of Fine Arts, and his firsthand experience of the 1930 Stockholm Exhibition had a decisive influence on his development.

*Sigvard Bernadotte, Pitcher, design intro-
duced 1952, triangular construction from
one piece of sterling silver, number 13.*

*Sigvard Bernadotte, Jug, design introduced
1938, sterling silver.*

When a Swedish department store wanted to launch a line of modern silverware, the youthful Bernadotte, among others, was recommended as a designer. The silversmith who was to execute the work was none other than Jørgen Jensen, Georg Jensen's second-eldest son, who at the time was living and working in Stockholm. Niels Wendel, the art dealer and partner in the Jensen company, recommended Sigvard Bernadotte to P. A. Pedersen, then engineer and general manager of the smithy, and in 1930 a contract was made in Copenhagen. Thus began a collaboration that, but for a few interruptions, was to last a quarter of a century.

Sigvard Bernadotte never concealed the fact that he was not overly fond of what had become known as the Georg Jensen style; yet, he cannot be classified as a functionalist. His designs for silverware introduced a modern Swedish taste that was to a degree alien to the Danish silver tradition. It was not, however, wholly new to the Danish public. Swedish design had already been introduced into Denmark by Britta Drewsen, Swedish by birth, who was the artistic adviser to Bo (a furniture company, now named Illums Bolighus).

Exports were of major importance to Georg Jensen, and Bernadotte's new silverwork served this purpose well, making its first appearance at exhibitions in London and New York. The most characteristic feature of Bernadotte's is a preference for geometrical figures, spheres, cylinders, and funnels, used together with a very moderate enrichment by engraved lines, profiles, and soldered parallel fluting. His style was elegant and distinctive, as was the artist himself.

World War II threatened stagnation. Connection with stores abroad was severed, and the flow of crude silver stopped. For the first time the smithy took up the manufacture of stainless steel, which was designed by Harald Nielsen among others, and silverwork had to be limited to inlays in wood or decoration on porcelain. In part through the unprecedented success enjoyed by the Kongemærket, an emblem designed by Arno Malinowski, however, employment was maintained fairly unimpaired until silver again became available a few years after the end of the war. It was not only silver that was eagerly awaited; innovation was also longed for. When the war ended in 1945 it was exactly ten years since Georg Jensen and Johan Rohde had passed away. The world had changed.

The post-war establishment of Georg Jensen was fortunate in having the engineer Anders Hostrup-Pedersen as general manager of the smithy with Harald Nielsen by his side; Gustav Pedersen and Henry Pilstrup, respectively, guaranteed the quality of the holloware and jewelry departments. It was further good fortune that the firm had been able to keep intact its staff of expert gold- and silversmiths.

The first eminent young artist to be attached to Georg Jensen after the war was Henning Koppel. At the time he was twenty-seven years old and had just returned from Sweden, where he had been a refugee during the German occupation of Denmark. In Stockholm the home-furnishing company Svenskt Tenn had asked him to design bracelets and necklaces to be made of pewter, a material to which Henning Koppel has reverted in recent years in his work for Georg Jensen. Henning Koppel's artistic education rested solidly on two foundations: he had been taught drawing by Bizzie Høyer, a now almost forgotten but highly respected and very demanding

*Henning Koppel, Bracelet, design introduced
1947, sterling silver.*

*Henning Koppel, Bowl, design introduced
1950, sterling silver.*

teacher, and he had studied sculpture under Professor Utzon-Frank at the Royal
Danish Academy of Fine Arts.

Continuing his work in jewelry begun for Svenskt Tenn, Koppel began designing
silver ornaments for Georg Jensen. Whereas his drawings and sculptures tended
toward naturalism, his silverwork, from the very outset, was abstract and sculptural. Some bracelets from around 1945 consist of chains made of differently shaped
individual links. Their inner and outer contours form a series of expressive, softly
rounded, waving shapes, joined together in an animated dancing chain. This jewelry was completely new in character, unlike anything made before. Koppel pursued
his formal ideas in a three-branched candlestick in which the branches at different
levels are connected by arched and bent rods, forming an imaginative whole reminiscent of a giant saurian bone.

When the import of silver in quantity was again possible, Henning Koppel began
a major holloware series, quite different from anything that had previously been
done at the Jensen silversmithy. He was given enthusiastic support by Harald Nielsen. The older artist had a sharp eye for the talent of the younger Koppel and taught
him many things concerning the possibilities of silver. Henning Koppel has always
acknowledged the importance of Nielsen's encouragement and support.

A master draftsman, Henning Koppel executed precise designs, which formed
the basis of his holloware. He also modeled in clay in order to understand the design three-dimensionally. The result was a line of jugs, bowls, and dishes that has
earned him the reputation of being the leading Danish silver craftsman and gained
him a reputation in many countries. In 1957 Koppel designed his famous set of
silver flatware, the Caravel pattern, perhaps the most handsome silver flatware
created in modern times.

He later transferred some of his personal and highly expressive forms to porcelain, executed for the Bing & Grondahl Porcelain Manufactory. Henning Koppel's
skills as a designer have also found expression in other kinds of work, including
chairs, a lamp, and stamps.

Somewhat later than Henning Koppel, the two architects Nanna and Jørgen
Ditzel began designing rings, bracelets, necklaces and other pieces of jewelry for
the Georg Jensen Silversmithy. In contrast to Koppel's extremely animated and
expressive jewelry with its links of differentiated thicknesses and turnings, the
Ditzel jewelry is simple with either convex or concave links. An individual piece of
jewelry subtly blends with finger, hand, or neck. Some of their work is executed in
gold and set with precious stones, for which the Ditzels prefer the cabochon cutting.
Their main effort, however, has been their work in silver.

Before Magnus Stephensen began designing for the Georg Jensen Silversmithy
in 1950, he had been attached to Kay Bojesen's workshop. As a very young journeyman, Bojesen worked in the small Jensen smithy at 36 Bredgade. Like many
other employees he was heavily influenced by the work of Georg Jensen himself
and continued in the original Jensen style even after having set up his own establishment. Kay Bojesen, however, was precisely twenty years younger than Jensen
and, therefore, more open to the new currents of classical and functional taste dom-

*Magnus Stephensen, Saucepan, design
introduced 1954, sterling silver*

*Søren Georg Jensen, Candelabrum, design
introduced 1959, hand-raised from one piece
of sterling silver, number 84.*

inating what was considered the best in artware in the years between the wars. His "smooth" silver style was introduced in the late 1920s and made its first museum appearance in Bojesen's great solo show at the Danish Museum of Decorative Art in 1938. A few years later he entered into collaboration with Magnus Stephensen.

Stephensen was a creative architect specializing in domestic architecture, but like many other gifted architects of his generation he was keenly interested in industrial design. He designed some holloware for Kay Bojesen, including a much admired teapot—its serviceable utility rivaled only by its sophisticated design carried out without profiles or ornament. Thus, it was obviously an experienced craftsman who found his place at the Georg Jensen Silversmithy. By and large Stephensen continued along the lines of the work he had created for Bojesen. He designed a series of holloware objects that by virtue of their beauty and consistent regard to detail, executed with faultless workmanship, constitute what may be called the most exquisite collection of modern Danish silver. Because of the nature of his education, Stephensen took a keen interest in the utility of objects, as is evident in his handle design. The combination of function and beauty in his work is reminiscent of the best in Japanese handicraft, a subject to which Magnus Stephensen dedicated an entire book.

Stephensen designed a set of stainless steel flatware with gently concave handles that merge into the bowl of the spoon and the prongs of the fork. He also designed a set of silver flatware. As was Henning Koppel, Magnus Stephensen was also interested in the porcelain industry and for a number of years collaborated with the Royal Copenhagen Porcelain Manufactory.

Many other artists and craftsmen at one time or another during the years after World War II worked for the Georg Jensen Silversmithy. Some are recorded in the pages that follow, but this brief history of the artists and craftsmen of the smithy would not be fairly representative without special mention of Søren Georg Jensen. He served his apprenticeship as a silversmith with the Jensen workshop and was awarded a silver medal for his diploma piece in 1936, one year after the death of his father. Subsequently he studied sculpture at the Royal Danish Academy of Fine Arts and graduated in 1945. His apprenticeship partly followed the pattern set by his father, but Søren Georg Jensen showed remarkable gifts as a sculptor. Even after 1949, when he was permanently attached to the Jensen silversmithy, he never relinquished his interest in sculpture. Nonetheless, Søren Georg Jensen dedicated most of his work to the design of silver holloware. He was fascinated by the possibilities of cylindrical form and with the cylinder as his point of departure designed a number of works—monumental even when of small size—that have great artistic strength. In several ways they amplify and elaborate the forms of his independent sculpture.

The name Georg Jensen, then, embodies several concepts of design extending over a number of years. The style of the founder underwent many modifications and changes. Yet underlying the constant change was a stable continuity, stemming from the concepts of Georg Jensen himself. One is tempted to say that the name stands not only for a sense of style and technical perfection, but connotes as well a dynasty.

ARTISTS AND
SELECTED DESIGNS

Objects are lent by the Georg Jensen
Sølvsmedie A/S, Copenhagen.
Dimensions are in millimeters.
Jensen production numbers are
given in brackets following object
identifications.

GUNDORPH ALBERTUS

Gundorph Albertus (1887-1970)
studied sculpture at the Royal
Danish Academy of Fine Arts. In
1911 he was employed as a chaser
by the Georg Jensen Silversmithy and from 1926 to 1954 he
served as the company's assistant
director. While at Georg Jensen's,
Albertus designed Mitra, the
company's first stainless steel
cutlery pattern in serial production. Albertus was represented in
many exhibitions and received a
gold medal at the Paris World Exhibition in 1925 and the Diplome
d'honneur at L'Exposition
Internationale in Paris in 1937.

1. *Vase* [465]
   Not illustrated
   design introduced 1936
   raised and chased sterling silver
   bowl and base
   height: 125 mm

2. *Strawberry Spoon, Cactus*
   Pattern [30]
   design introduced 1930
   sterling silver with hand-drilled
   and engraved motif on bowl
   length: 260 mm

VILHELM ALBERTUS

Vilhelm Albertus (1878-1963),
brother of Gundorph Albertus,
worked for many years in the
design department of the Georg
Jensen Silversmithy.

3. *Brooch* [296]
    design introduced 1942
    stamped and hand-soldered
    sterling silver
    width: 30 mm

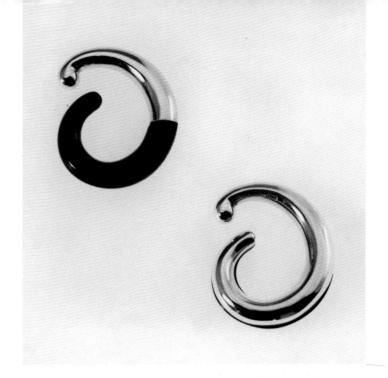

ANNE AMMITZBØLL

Anne Ammitzbøll (born 1934) studied at the Finn Juhl School of Interior Design and Mulle Høyrup's experimental school for textile printing in Kokkedal, Denmark. She has designed and sold children's clothes in her own shop and has been employed as a designer of leather goods by Form & Farve in Copenhagen. Ammitzbøll has worked with Andreas Mikkelsen since 1970 and has been employed as a designer by the Georg Jensen Silversmithy since 1978.

4. *Earrings [A33]*
    design introduced 1972
    cast and sculpted sterling silver,
    mounted with carnelian
    width: 27 mm

5. *Table Lighter [400]*
    design introduced 1979
    cone-shaped construction from
    one piece of sterling silver,
    soldered top and bottom
    height: 77 mm

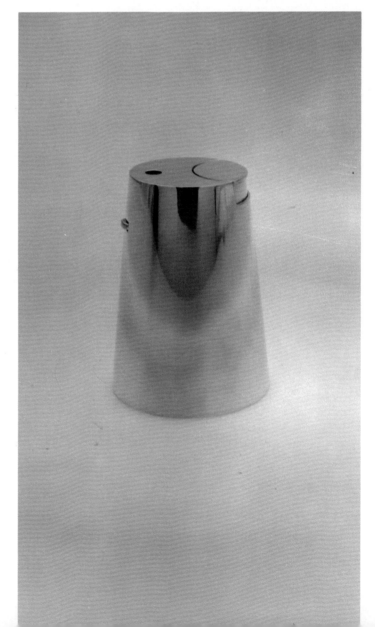

IB JUST ANDERSEN

After working with Georg Jensen,
Ib Just Andersen (1884-1943)
set up his own company, Just
Andersen Pewter, in 1918.

6. *Cutlery, Bloch Pattern [46]*
   design introduced 1934
   forged and hand-polished
   sterling silver with stainless steel
   blade
   fork length: 180 mm
   knife length: 220 mm
   spoon length: 190 mm

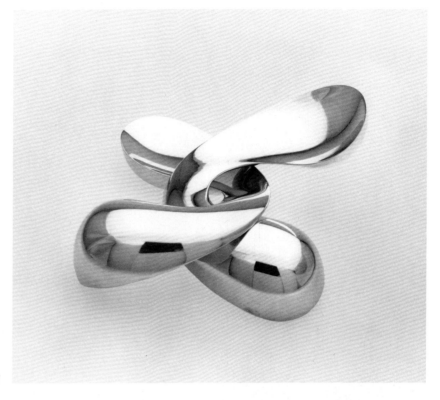

KNUD HOLST ANDERSEN

After completing his apprenticeship as a silversmith in Denmark in 1961, Knud Holst Andersen (born 1935) went abroad to continue his studies at the Tokyo University of Art from 1961 to 1964 and the Royal College of Art in Kensington, England, in 1975. Andersen has submitted examples of his silver and bronze holloware to exhibitions held in Denmark, Sweden, Germany, and France. His work is represented in museums and other public collections and has won for him many honors. In 1973 the Danish Society of Arts and Crafts named him "Artist-Craftsman of the Year." He has been associated with the Georg Jensen Silversmithy since 1973.

7. *Sculpture*, Fable [3]
design introduced 1974
hand-raised and joined
sterling silver
width: 150 mm

RIGMOR ANDERSEN

After studying architecture at the Royal Danish Academy of Fine Arts, Rigmor Andersen (born 1903) worked with the Danish architect Kaare Klint from 1929 to 1939. She has taught at the Danish academy since 1944. Examples of her work are in the collections of many museums, including the Danish Museum of Decorative Art in Copenhagen. The Knud V. Englehardt Memorial Prize and the Eckersberg Medal (received with Annelise Bjørner) have been awarded to Andersen.

ANNELISE BJØRNER

Annelise Bjørner (born 1932) studied architecture and industrial design at the Royal Danish Academy of Fine Arts. She has worked with architects Arne Karlsen, Vilhelm Wohlert, and Mogens Koch. Since 1962 Bjørner has collaborated with Rigmor Andersen with whom she received the Eckersberg Medal in 1968 for the Margrethe cutlery pattern.

8. *Cutlery, Margrethe Pattern*
   [134]
   design introduced 1966
   forged and hand-polished
   sterling silver with stainless steel
   blades
   salad fork length: 165 mm
   fork length: 170 mm
   knife length: 225 mm, each
   soup spoon length: 162 mm
   teaspoon length: 146 mm

STEFFEN ANDERSEN

From 1956 until 1958 Steffen
Andersen (born 1936) attended
the Danish College of Jewelry,
Silversmithing, and Commercial
Design (Guldsmedehoejskolen).
He has worked with the Georg
Jensen Silversmithy in London
from 1959 to 1960 and in
Copenhagen in the design
department from 1961 to 1971, in
the advertising department from
1971 to 1975, and in the holloware
department since 1975.

9. *Necklace* [210]
    design introduced 1969
    pressed, hand-soldered, and
    finished sterling silver
    length: 406 mm

JENS ANDREASEN

Jens Andreasen (born 1924)
studied at the Royal Danish
Academy of Fine Arts in
Copenhagen. His work is
represented in the Metropolitan
Museum of Art in New York,
the National Museum in Copenhagen, and in museums in
Szczecin and Gdansk, Poland.
He has been associated with
the Georg Jensen Silversmithy
since 1978.

10. *Sculpture [1216]*
    design introduced 1979
    hand-raised and joined sterling
    silver
    width: 330 mm

SIGVARD
BERNADOTTE

Son of Gustav Adolf VI, king of
Sweden, and brother of Ingrid,
queen mother of Denmark, Count
Sigvard Bernadotte (born 1907)
entered the Royal Swedish
Academy of Fine Arts in 1929
and in 1930 began working for
the Georg Jensen Silversmithy.
With Acton Bjørn and other
designers, Bernadotte has been
responsible for many industrial
designs. From the beginning of
his association with the Georg
Jensen Silversmithy, his clear-cut
disciplined forms — drawing
heavily on established Swedish
traditions — were in many ways a
break with what had until then
been part of the concept of
Georg Jensen silver. As a member
of the board of directors for the
Georg Jensen Silversmithy,
Bernadotte has greatly influenced
the style and reputation of the
firm.

11. *Carving Fork, Knife, and Spit*
   [14]
   design introduced 1939
   two sterling silver pieces,
   soldered together with stainless
   steel blades
   fork length: 310 mm
   knife length: 335 mm
   spit length: 210 mm

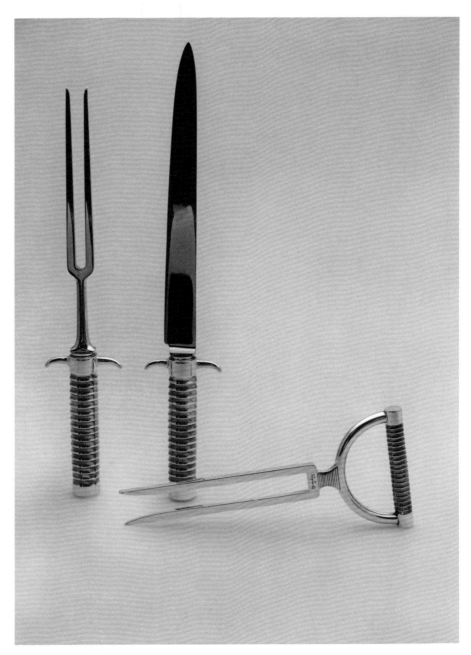

12. *Bowl [856A]*
    design introduced 1939
    spun and hand-chased
    sterling silver
    diameter: 255 mm

13. *Pitcher [1010]*
    Illustrated on page 18
    design introduced 1952
    triangular construction from
    one piece of sterling silver
    height: 172 mm

14. *Candlesticks [855B]*
    design introduced 1938
    spun, soldered, and hand-
    engraved sterling silver
    height: 250 mm

IB BLUITGEN

After serving an apprenticeship
at the Georg Jensen Silversmithy, Ib Bluitgen (born 1921)
studied sculpture at the Royal
Danish Academy of Fine Arts
from 1945 to 1948. He was
employed in the design department of the Georg Jensen Silversmithy from 1948 until 1961.
Since then he has made silver
holloware and jewelry in his own
workshop.

15. *Box [332]*
     design introduced 1953; no longer
     produced
     hand-sculpted sterling silver
     height: 40 mm

BENTE BONNÉ

Bente Bonné (born 1929) is a
Danish glass engraver.

16. *Bracelet [120]*
     design introduced 1960
     pressed, soldered, and enameled
     sterling silver
     length: 180 mm

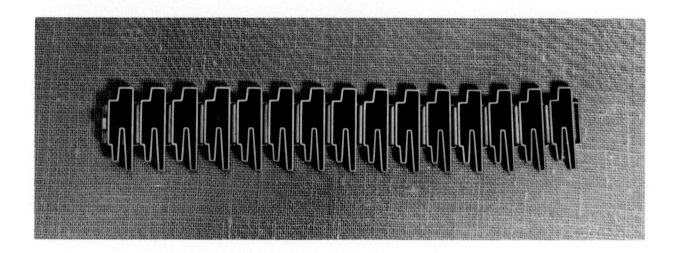

MAX BRAMMER

After training as a silversmith at
the Jensen silverworks, Max
Brammer (born 1940) opened his
own workshop in 1961.

17. *Pendant [155]*
     design introduced 1976
     cast and forged sterling silver
     with moss agate
     length: 90 mm

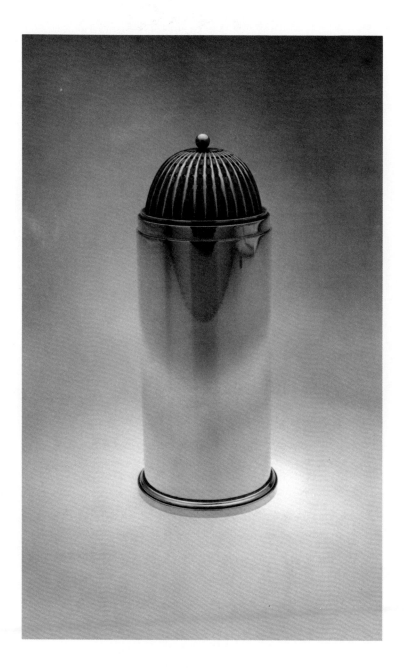

OVE BRØBECK

Ove Brøbeck (died 1971) worked
for many years in the design
departments of Oscar Gundlach-
Pedersen and Georg Jensen.

18. *Sugar Caster* [627]
     design introduced 1931
     spun, hand-chased, and drilled
     sterling silver
     height: 146 mm

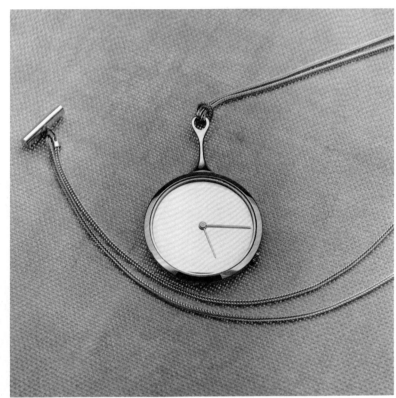

TORUN BÜLOW-HÜBE

After training in her native Sweden, Torun Bülow-Hübe (born 1927) moved to France in 1956 and lived in Paris and in the village of Biot on the Riviera for eleven years. She now lives on the island of Java, where she has undertaken a wide range of design projects, including the design of kitchen utensils, textiles, baskets, lamps, and office equipment. She has won many awards, including the Lunning Prize and a gold medal at the 1960 Milan Triennale. She has produced work for the Georg Jensen Silversmithy since 1967.

19. *Watch* [225]
    design introduced 1977
    stainless steel with sterling silver chain
    diameter: 33 mm

20. *Brooch* [374]
    design introduced 1969
    pressed and hand-shaped sterling silver
    diameter: 70 mm

21. *Oval Neckring* [904]
    Not illustrated
    design introduced 1970
    drawn 18k gold, fitted with pearls
    diameter: 150 mm

JØRGEN DAHLERUP

Trained as a silversmith, Jørgen
Dahlerup (born 1930) studied
sculpture and industrial design
at the Royal Danish Academy of
Fine Arts. His work, which
includes holloware and religious
objects, is represented in the
Bodo Glaub Collection in
Cologne, Germany, and in the
Danish Museum of Decorative
Art and the Danish Design
Center in Copenhagen.

GERT HOLBEK

A pipemaker, designer, and
inventor, Gert Holbek (born
1928) worked with Jørgen
Dahlerup on the design of the
Prism cutlery pattern.

22. *Cutlery, Prism Pattern* [315]
    design introduced 1969
    *forged and hand-polished
    stainless steel
    fork length: 179 mm
    knife length: 210 mm
    spoon length: 200 mm*

IBE DAHLQUIST

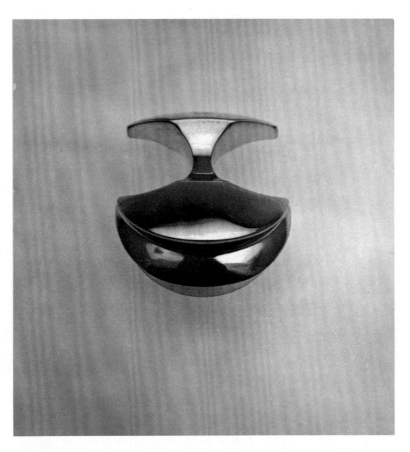

An artist who has had many
exhibitions in Sweden and
elsewhere, Ibe Dahlquist (born
1924) studied at the Swedish
School of Arts, Crafts, and
Design in Stockholm. Her work
is on display in Goldsmiths' Hall,
London, and in many Swedish
museums. She maintains her
own workshop in Stockholm and
since 1965 has designed jewelry
for the Georg Jensen Silversmithy.

23. *Ring [161]*
design introduced 1970
cast sterling silver
diameter: 38 mm

24. *Armring [unique object]*
     designed 1969
     cast and hand-sculpted sterling
     silver
     diameter: 97 mm

28. *Necklace* [1159]
design introduced 1966
pressed, stamped, and hand-bent
18k gold
length: 406 mm

25. *Armring* [121]
design introduced 1960
each link made of two sterling
silver halves, soldered together
diameter: 95 mm

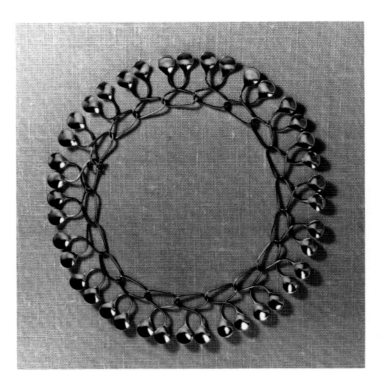

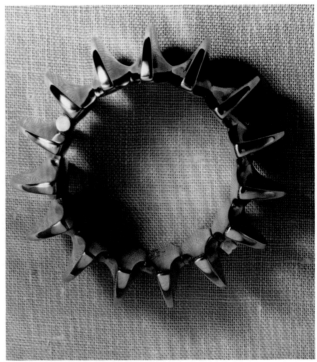

NANNA DITZEL

After studying at the Danish School of Arts, Crafts, and Design in Copenhagen, Nanna Ditzel (born 1923) started her own design firm in 1946. Ditzel received first prize in a competition organized by the Goldsmiths' Guild in 1950, the Lunning Prize in 1956, and a gold medal at the Milan Triennale in 1960. Since 1970 she has maintained a design firm and showroom in London, where she displays furniture, textiles, jewelry, and porcelain of her own design. Her work has been exhibited at the Metropolitan Museum of Art in New York, the Danish Museum of Decorative Art in Copenhagen, and the Louvre in Paris. She has been associated with the Georg Jensen Silversmithy since 1954.

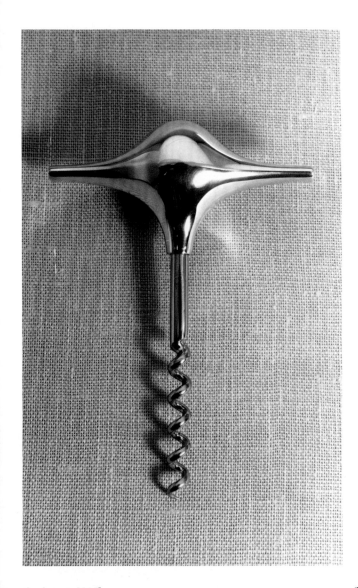

26. *Corkscrew* [135]
    design introduced 1958
    handle pressed in two sterling
    silver pieces, soldered together
    length: 120 mm

27. *Ring* [91]
    Not illustrated
    design introduced 1955
    pressed sterling silver
    diameter: 29 mm

29. *Armring* [1111]
    design introduced 1956
    handmade and soldered 18k gold
    diameter: 100 mm

TIAS ECKHOFF

A graduate of the Norwegian
School of Arts and Crafts, Tias
Eckhoff (born 1926) has since
1949 been employed by the
Porsgrund Porcelain Factory in
Norway, first as a designer and
later in 1953 as an art director.
Eckhoff has received many prizes,
including the Lunning Prize in
1953 and gold medals at the
Milan Triennale in 1954 and 1957.

30. *Cutlery, Cypress Pattern* [99]
    design introduced 1953
    forged and hand-polished
    sterling silver with stainless
    steel blades
    salad fork length: 170 mm
    fork length: 190 mm
    knife length: 220 mm
    soup spoon length: 180 mm
    teaspoon length: 153 mm
    butter knife length: 158 mm

FLEMMING ESKILDSEN

After training as a silversmith
at the Georg Jensen Silversmithy, Flemming Eskildsen
(born 1930) joined the firm in
1958.

31. *Pipe Tamper [401]*
     Not illustrated
     design introduced 1979
     cast sterling silver
     length: 76 mm

32. *Necklace [125]*
     design introduced 1961
     cast, soldered, and hand-
     polished sterling silver
     length: 406 mm

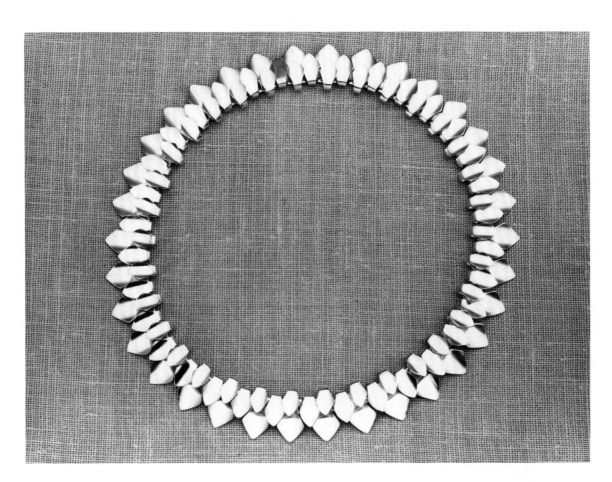

TUK FISCHER Trained as a goldsmith, Tuk Fischer (born 1939) attended the Danish School of Arts, Crafts, and Design in 1964. She began working as a designer at the Georg Jensen Silversmithy in 1962.

33. *Necklace* [133]
design introduced 1963
pressed, soldered, and hand-polished sterling silver
length: 406 mm

ASTRID FOG

Astrid Fog (born 1911) created her first collection of jewelry for the Georg Jensen Silversmithy in 1969. She also designs clothes and lamps and has for many years been affiliated with the Royal Copenhagen Porcelain Manufactory.

34.   *Ring [166]*
        design introduced 1971
        hand-shaped sterling silver,
        mounted with green onyx
        diameter: 34 mm

35.   *Armring [235]*
        design introduced 1971
        spun ring with cast sterling
        silver drops
        diameter: 70 mm

ERNST FORSMANN

Ernst Forsmann (born 1910) completed his training as a goldsmith when he was twenty years old. He was associated with the Georg Jensen Silversmithy from 1953 to 1975.

36. *Necklace* [191]
design introduced 1969
pressed, hinged, and hand-finished sterling silver
length: 400 mm

KIRSTEN FOURNAIS

Kirsten Fournais (born 1933) has
designed jewelry for the Georg
Jensen Silversmithy since 1978.

37. *Buttons [134, 135, 136, 137]*
     designs introduced 1979
     cast sterling silver
     diameter: 20 mm, each

BENT GABRIELSEN

Bent Gabrielsen (born 1928)
attended the Danish College of
Jewelry, Silversmithing, and
Commercial Design from 1950 to
1953. He was awarded the
Lunning Prize in 1964 and a gold
medal at the Milan Triennale
in 1960.

38. *Necklace* [115]
design introduced 1959
*cast and assembled sterling
silver*
length: 406 mm

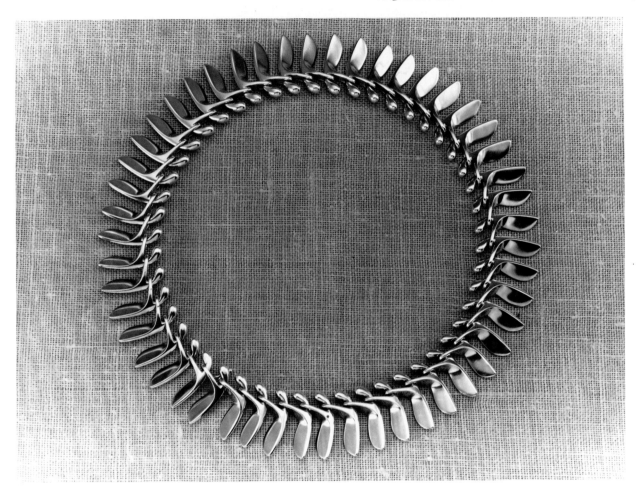

BERTEL GARDBERG

A Finnish silversmith, Bertel
Gardberg (born 1916) worked in
Copenhagen before setting up
his own practice in Helsinki. He
has worked for Galerie Lafayette
in Paris and the Kilkenny Design
Workshops in Ireland. In 1961
he received the Lunning Prize.

39. *Cuff Links* [892]
    design introduced 1966
    cast and hand-engraved 18k gold
    center with hand-constructed
    18k gold frame
    width: 15 mm

40. *Cuff Links* [893]
    design introduced 1966
    cast and hand-engraved 18k gold
    center with hand-constructed
    18k gold frame
    width: 17 mm

ARJE GRIEGST

After training in Copenhagen,
Arje Griegst (born 1938) studied
in Rome and Paris. From 1963
to 1965 he was a professor at the
Bezalel Academy of Arts and
Design in Jerusalem. He has
designed ceramics for the Royal
Copenhagen Porcelain Manufac-
tory and has worked with the Georg
Jensen Silversmithy since 1965.

41. *Ring* [11]
     design introduced 1965
     free-form cast 18k gold
     diameter: 28 mm

OSCAR GUNDLACH-PEDERSEN

After completing his architectural training at the Royal Danish Academy of Fine Arts, Oscar Gundlach-Pedersen (1886-1960) participated in a number of exhibitions held in Copenhagen during the 1920s and '30s. A designer of many prominent buildings in Denmark, Gundlach-Pedersen was manager of the Georg Jensen Silversmithy from 1927 until 1931.

42. *Cutlery, Nordic Pattern* [76]
design introduced 1937
forged and hand-polished sterling silver with stainless steel blade
fork length: 180 mm
knife length: 230 mm
spoon length: 190 mm

POUL HANSEN   Now retired from the Georg
Jensen Silversmithy, Poul
Hansen (born 1902) started
working with Jensen in 1922 and
was appointed foreman of the
goldsmith workshop in 1937.

43.   *Ring* [124]
     design introduced 1968
     cast sterling silver ring with
     hand-mounted onyx
     diameter: 13 mm

44.   *Cuff Links* [75A]
     design introduced 1955
     pressed sterling silver button with
     handmade sterling silver link
     width: 24 mm

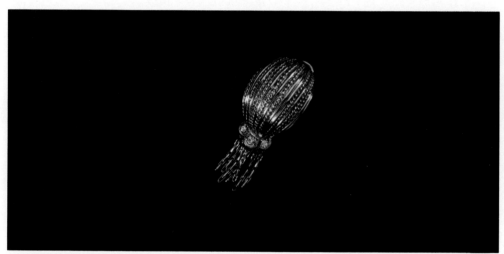

PER HARILD

After training as a silversmith in Denmark, Per Harild (born 1934) traveled to Germany in 1955 to further his studies. In the mid-sixties he designed gold jewelry for the Georg Jensen Silver-smithy. Today he has his own workshop.

45. *Ring [863A]*
    design introduced 1966
    cast 18k gold ring with assembled 18k gold chains, mounted with diamonds
    diameter: 19 mm

MARIE HASSENPFLUG

German-born Marie Hassenpflug (born 1933) studied metalwork for seven years at the School of Arts and Crafts (Die Werk Kunstschule) in Krefeld, Germany, and later spent four years studying enameling at the School of Arts and Crafts in Düsseldorf. In 1961 she opened her own workshop in Düsseldorf. She has been affiliated with the Georg Jensen Silversmithy since 1971.

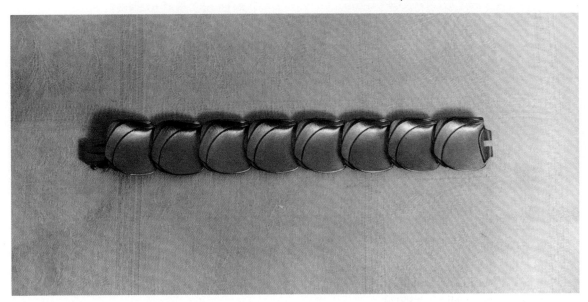

46. *Bracelet* [959]
     design introduced 1974
     cast and hinged 18k gold links
     length: 176 mm

HENRY HEERUP

The work of Henry Heerup (born 1907), a Danish painter, sculptor, and graphics designer, has been displayed in museums in Denmark, Sweden, and the United States. He has received many awards, including the Eckersberg Medal in 1958 and the Thorvaldsen Medal in 1967. He received honorary membership in the Royal Danish Academy of Fine Arts in 1977.

47. *Pendant* [150]
    design introduced 1974
    pressed and hand-enameled
    sterling silver
    width: 60 mm

PIET HEIN The Danish author and inventor Piet Hein (born 1905) has frequently written on the relationship between art and science. In tackling a town-planning project in 1959 involving Sergels Torg (a plaza in Stockholm), Hein introduced the "superellipse," a concept that has been used to solve many other design problems. His awards include the Aarestrup Medal and the Alexander Graham Bell Silver Bell, which he received in 1968. He was awarded an honorary doctorate from Yale University in 1972. Under the pen name "Kumbel" he has written hundreds of "grooks," such as: I'd like to know/what this whole show/is all about/before it's out.

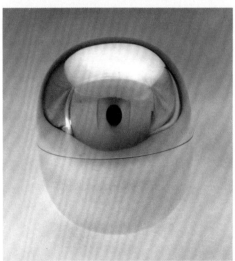

48. *Tray [1146A]*
    design introduced 1966
    raised from one sheet of sterling silver
    width x depth: 248 x 189 mm

49. *Box, Superegg [1147A]*
    design introduced 1966
    spun in two tight fitting halves of sterling silver
    height: 100 mm

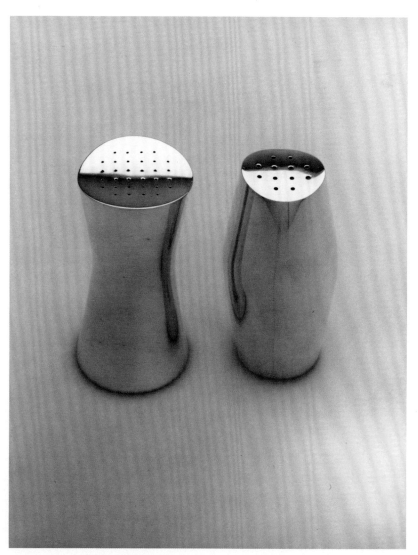

HANS HENRIKSEN

Educated at the Royal Danish Academy of Fine Arts, Hans Henriksen (born 1921) directed his own design firm from 1958 until 1968. He has been employed by the Danish Broadcasting and Television Corporation since 1963.

50. *Salt and Pepper Shakers* [1031]
     design introduced 1954
     hand-raised and joined sterling silver
     height: 80 mm

GUDMUND HENTZE   After studying painting at the Royal Danish Academy of Fine Arts, Gudmund Hentze (1875-1948) exhibited his work in Denmark and other European countries. He designed objects in pewter and silver for the companies of Mogens Ballin, A. Michelsen, and Georg Jensen.

51.   *Brooch [55]*
      design introduced 1910
      pressed sterling silver, mounted with green agate in handmade frame
      width: 60 mm

ERIK HERLØW

A graduate of the Royal Danish
Academy of Fine Arts, Erik
Herløw (born 1913) has participated in a wide range of design
projects; he was one of the
architects for the American
embassy built in Copenhagen in
1954. Interested in applied art,
Herløw has designed many
official Danish exhibition
pavilions and installations,
including those for the Danish
exhibition at the 1951 Milan
Triennale; "Design in Scandi-
navia," a traveling exhibition
shown in twenty-five North
American museums in 1954; and
"Formes Scandinaves," an
exhibition held at the Musée des
Arts Décoratifs in Paris in 1958.
He has served as artistic
consultant to the Royal Copenhagen Porcelain Manufactory
since 1955 and professor of
industrial design at the Royal
Danish Academy of Fine Arts
since 1959. He was awarded gold
medals at the Milan Triennale in
1954 and 1957 and the Eckersberg
Medal in 1958.

52. *Brooch* [802]
     design introduced 1960
     18k gold with hand mounted
     tourmaline
     height x width: 40 x 45 mm

53. *Ring* [804]
     Not illustrated
     design introduced 1960
     cast and sculpted 18k gold with
     amethyst
     diameter: 14 mm

KNUD HOLSCHER

Knud Holscher (born 1930) studied architecture at the Royal Danish Academy of Fine Arts. Winner of many architectural competitions and design awards, Holscher has received the Eckersberg Medal in 1970 and the ID Prize of the Society of International Design. Since 1967 he has been a partner in the design firm of Krohn & Hartvig Rasmussen and since 1968 he has been a professor of architecture at the Royal Danish Academy of Fine Arts.

54. *Salad Spoon and Fork* [*3102*]
     design introduced 1975
     bent stainless steel wires
     spoon length: 310 mm
     fork length: 310 mm

55. *Ice Tongs* [*3108*]
     design introduced 1975
     bent stainless steel wires
     length: 300 mm

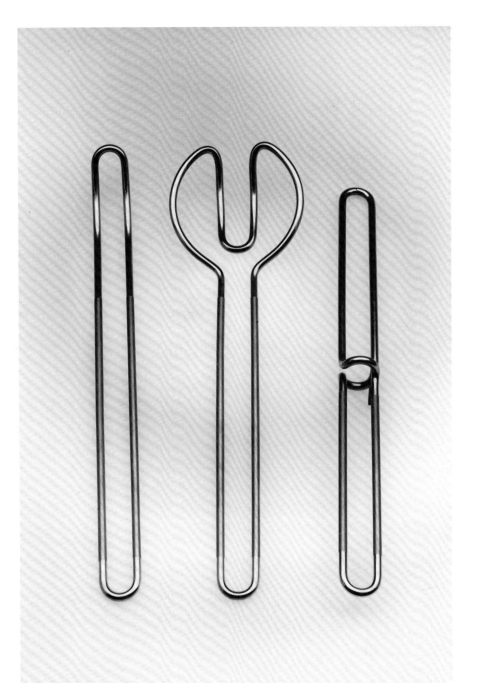

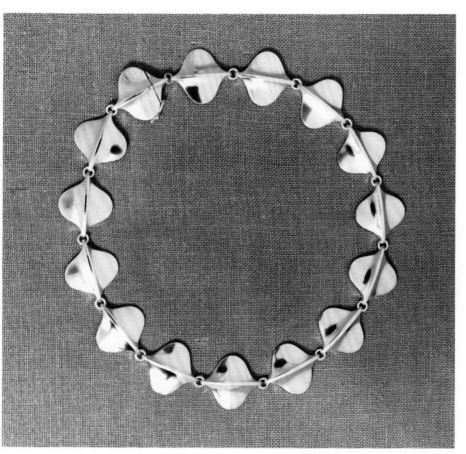

ANNETTE HOWDLE

Trained at the Jensen silverworks and the Danish College of Jewelry, Silversmithing, and Commercial Design, Annette Howdle (born 1938) was employed by the Jensen design department from 1962 until 1968. She now resides in England.

56. *Necklace* [176]
    design introduced 1967
    pressed sterling silver links with
    handmade sterling silver clasp
    length: 406 mm

THERESIA HVORSLEV

Educated at the School of
Industrial Design in Stockholm,
Theresia Hvorslev (born 1935)
has received several international
awards. Preferring to work with
silver, she designs holloware,
jewelry, and cutlery.

57. *Coasters [1099, 1100]*
     designs introduced 1961
     raised sterling silver
     diameter: 95 mm, left; *100 mm*,
     right

OLE ISHØJ

Trained at the Jensen silverworks, Ole Ishøj (born 1942)
worked with Andreas Mikkelsen
from 1972 until 1978. He has
designed jewelry for the Georg
Jensen Silversmithy since 1978.

58. *Armrings [A7A, A7B]*
    designs introduced 1973
    handcut and hammered sterling
    silver
    diameter: 62 mm, each

59. *Rings [A1077A, A1077B]*
    designs introduced 1973
    18k gold
    height: 17 mm, each

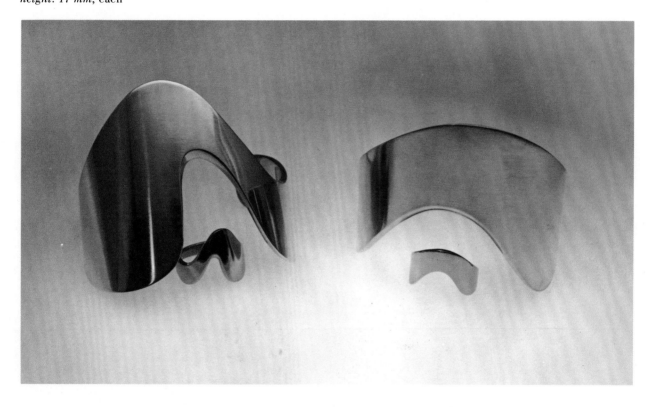

HANS ITTIG

Hans Ittig (born 1933) maintains
a workshop in Switzerland, his
native country.

60. *Bracelet* [829]
    design introduced 1961
    hinged and handcut 18k gold
    links, mounted with tourmaline
    length: 176 mm

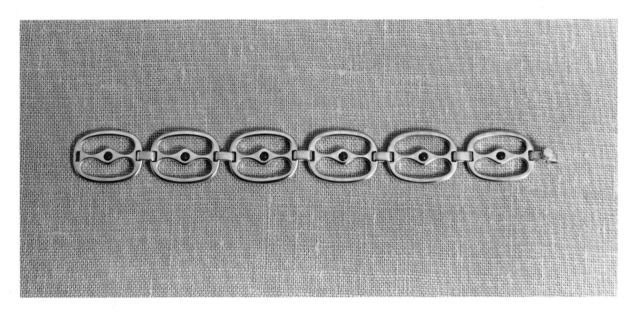

AXEL JENSEN

Trained as a silversmith, Axel
Jensen (born 1916) first worked
at the Georg Jensen Silversmithy
from 1936 to 1940. He maintained his own workshop from
1940 until 1949, and since 1950
he has been employed in the
Jensen modelmaking workshop.

61. *Bracelet* [296]
     design introduced 1978
     cast sterling silver links,
     mounted with coral
     length: 176 mm

GEORG JENSEN   Upon completion of his apprenticeship as a goldsmith in 1887, Georg Jensen (1866-1935) entered the Royal Danish Academy of Fine Arts, graduating as a sculptor in 1892. He began making ceramics in 1898 in a workshop outside Copenhagen with Christian Joachim (who later became director of the Royal Copenhagen Porcelain Manufactory). In 1904 Jensen opened a small silversmithy that quickly attracted a group of innovative artists including Johan Rohde, who was to become one of Jensen's leading patrons and designers.

Georg Jensen influenced his craft in two important ways: he reestablished and maintained professional traditions, and he insisted on only the highest artistic standards.

62. *Teapot [2A]*
    Illustrated on page 14
    design introduced 1905
    pot spun in two sterling silver
    pieces, cast feet individually
    chased, blossom decoration and
    ivory handle individually shaped
    height: 105 mm

63. *Tray [159]*
    design introduced 1912
    hand-raised, chased, and
    hammered sterling silver
    width x depth: 320 x 222 mm

64. *Candelabrum [383A]*
    design introduced 1920
    spun and chased sterling silver
    base and handle, and hand-
    chased arms
    height: 265 mm

65. *Easter Egg* [unique object]
    designed 1908
    hand-raised, chased, and
    soldered sterling silver with
    amber and onyx
    width: 115 mm

66. *Sugar Caster* [159]
    design introduced 1912
    raised and chased sterling silver
    top, center, and base with drilled
    and cut motifs
    height: 190 mm

67. *Tea Machine* [182]
    design introduced 1915
    hand-raised sterling silver pot
    and burner, chased details, and
    ebony
    height: 310 mm

GEORG JENSEN

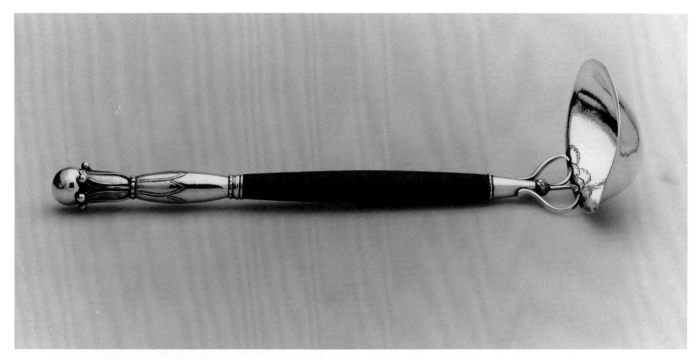

68. *Bowl [263B]*
    design introduced 1918
    spun sterling silver bowl, hand-
    chased sterling silver stem, and
    individually sculpted grape
    decorations
    height: 203 mm

69. *Dish with Cover [408B]*
    Not illustrated
    design introduced 1921
    raised sterling silver bottom and
    lid, chased sterling silver orna-
    ments, and individually sculpted
    grape decorations
    height x width: 165 x 265 mm

70. *Soup Ladle [66]*
    design introduced 1916
    sterling silver bowl and ebony
    handle, individually sculpted,
    soldered together on ebony
    center
    length: 432 mm

71. *Cutlery, Blossom Pattern* [84]
    design introduced 1919
    forged sterling silver with
    individually sculpted blossom
    leaf decorations with stainless
    steel blade
    fork length: 190 mm
    knife length: 240 mm
    spoon length: 197 mm

72. *Cutlery, Continental Pattern* [4]
    Illustrated on page 14
    design introduced 1908
    forged, hand-hammered, and
    polished sterling silver
    fork length: 185 mm
    knife length: 227 mm
    spoon length: 190 mm

73. *Fish Fork and Knife*
    design introduced 1904
    hand-forged and chased sterling
    silver
    fork length: 187 mm
    knife length: 195 mm

74. *Jam Spoon* [41/161]
    design introduced 1916
    hand-forged, cut, and finished
    sterling silver
    length: 190 mm

GEORG JENSEN

75. *Buckle* [9]
    Illustrated on page 12
    design introduced circa 1910
    hand-chased and cut sterling
    silver, mounted with garnets
    width: 120 mm

76. *Buckle* [41]
    design introduced 1910
    hand-chased and cut sterling
    silver, mounted with amber and
    garnet
    width: 120 mm

77. *Back Comb* [52]
    design introduced 1908
    hand-chased and cut sterling
    silver, mounted with amber and
    green agate
    length: 110 mm

78. *Ring* [18]
    design introduced 1905
    hand-chased and cut sterling
    silver, mounted with green agate
    diameter: 35 mm

79. *Earrings* [11]
    design introduced 1907
    hand-chased and cut sterling
    silver, mounted with amber
    length: 68 mm

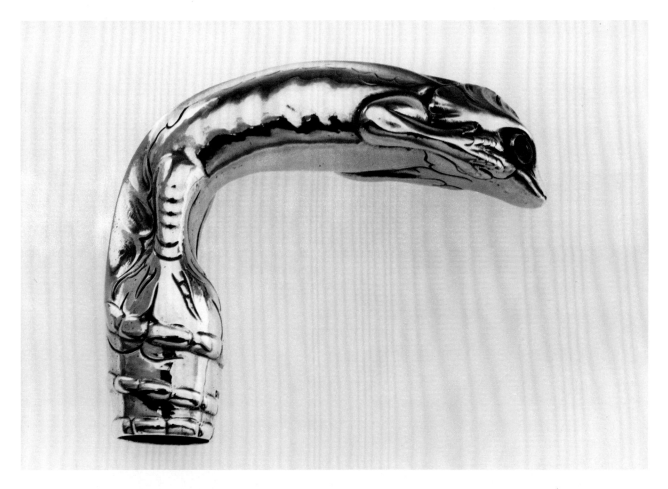

80. *Cane Handle [116]*
     design introduced 1919
     hand-raised, chased, and shaped
     sterling silver with green agate
     length: 110 mm approx.

JØRGEN JENSEN

Jørgen Jensen (1895-1966) studied silversmithing in Munich with Leonhard Ebert in 1914 and maintained his own workshop in Stockholm from 1923 to 1936. He designed silver holloware and jewelry while employed in the design department of the Georg Jensen Silversmithy from 1936 until 1962.

81. *Pitcher* [947]
     design introduced 1948
     spun sterling silver bottom,
     raised sterling silver top and
     handle
     height: 190 mm

SØREN GEORG JENSEN

Georg Jensen's second-youngest
son, Søren (born 1917), was
educated as a silversmith and
sculptor. In 1946 he received a
travel scholarship from the Royal
Danish Academy of Fine Arts
and in 1957 he received a
UNESCO scholarship that
enabled him to study in Italy. He
headed the design department of
the Georg Jensen Silversmithy
from 1962 until 1974. He has
received many awards, including
a gold medal at the Milan Triennale in 1960, the Eckersberg
Medal in 1966, and the Thorvaldsen Medal in 1974. His
sculptures are exhibited in
many museums, including the
Louisiana Museum near
Copenhagen.

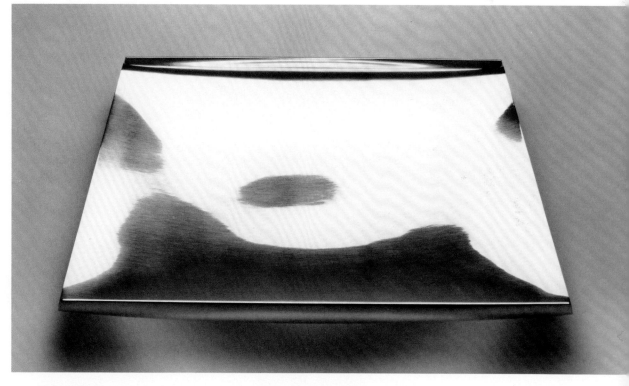

82. *Bracelet* [97]
    design introduced 1949
    hinged, cast, and chased sterling
    silver links with handmade
    sterling silver clasp
    length: 200 mm

83. *Dish* [1086]
    design introduced 1960
    hand-raised from one piece of
    sterling silver
    width x depth: 456 x 335 mm

84. *Candelabrum* [1087]
    Illustrated on page 20
    design introduced 1959
    hand-raised from one piece of
    sterling silver
    height: 176 mm

BJARNE JESPERSEN

Trained as an architect, Bjarne Jespersen (born 1947) has since 1971 been curator of David's Samling, a museum in Copenhagen. He designs silver sculptures for Georg Jensen Silversmithy and carves wood sculptures, which he frequently exhibits.

85. *Sculpture, Key [1258]*
     design introduced 1979
     cast sterling silver
     width: 50 mm

86. *Sculpture, Globe [1255]*
     design introduced 1979
     cast and hand-shaped sterling
     silver
     width: 40 mm

EDVARD KINDT-LARSEN

The designer Edvard Kindt-
Larsen (born 1901) has worked
chiefly on projects involving
exhibitions and industrial design.
From 1945 to 1953 he was prin-
cipal of the Danish School of
Arts, Crafts, and Design in
Copenhagen.

87. *Bracelet* [1103]
     design introduced 1952
     cast 18k gold links, hinged with
     handmade clasp
     length: 178 mm

HENNING KOPPEL

Henning Koppel (born 1918) was educated as a sculptor and designer at the Royal Danish Academy of Fine Arts in Copenhagen and at the Académie Ranson in Paris. He has been associated with the Georg Jensen Silversmithy since 1945, the Bing & Grøndahl Porcelain Manufactory since 1961, and the Orrefors Glassworks since 1971. His drawings and works in silver, porcelain, and glass are represented in museum collections throughout the world. His many awards include the Lunning Prize in 1953; gold medals at the Milan Triennale in 1951, 1954, and 1957; the International Design Award of the American Institute of Interior Designers in 1963; and the ID Prize of the Society of International Design for the stainless steel tableware he designed for the Jensen company in 1966. Regarded as one of this century's major designers of holloware and an innovator in the art of silverwork, Koppel has designed objects whose sweeping lines and smooth surfaces represent a departure from traditional forms in silver.

88. *Pitcher* [992]
design introduced 1952
hand-raised and sculpted
sterling silver
height: 287 mm

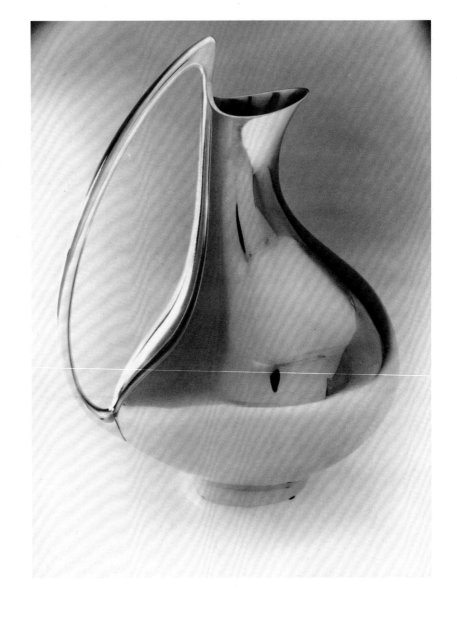

89.   *Dish with Cover* [1054]
      design introduced 1954
      hand-raised and sculpted
      sterling silver
      width x depth: 715 x 190 mm

90. *Tea Pot* [1043]
     design introduced 1954
     spun and raised sterling silver
     with handcut ivory
     height: 118 mm

91. *Desk Set*
    design introduced 1978
    sterling silver

    Pencil Cup [1243]
    height: 80 mm

    Pad Tray [1233]
    width x depth: 170 x 126 mm

    Letter Tray [1234]
    width x depth: 330 x 245 mm

    Clock [1230]
    height: 80 mm

    Box [1236A]
    diameter: 87 mm

    Box [1236B]
    diameter: 70 mm

Box [1236C]
diameter: 55 mm

Magnifying Glass [392]
length: 198 mm

Letter Opener [393]
length: 215 mm

Letter Weight [1231]
diameter: 65 mm

Pencil Tray [1232]
width x depth: 208 x 90 mm

Ruler [394]
length: 300 mm

92. *Cutlery, Caravel Pattern [111]*
    design introduced 1957
    forged and hand-polished
    sterling silver with stainless steel
    blades
    soup ladle length: 335 mm
    teaspoon length: 150 mm
    butter knife length: 155 mm
    salad fork length: 160 mm
    salad serving-spoon length:
    290 mm
    salad serving-fork length: 290 mm
    fork length: 190 mm
    knife length: 220 mm
    soup spoon length: 195 mm

93. *Bracelet* [88A]
     design introduced 1946
     cast and individually shaped
     sterling silver links
     length: 178 mm

94. *Box* [42]
     design introduced 1978
     pewter with ebony
     diameter: 70 mm

95. *Bowl* [28]
     Not illustrated
     design introduced 1978
     spun pewter
     height x width x depth:
     42 x 150 x 123 mm

96. *Candle Snuffer with Rest* [9]
    design introduced 1978
    pewter with ebony
    length: 235 mm

97. *Carving Fork and Knife* [405]
    design introduced 1971; tempo-
    rarily deleted from production
    forged stainless steel
    length: 310 mm, each

OLE KORTZAU

Working exclusively with textiles, graphics, porcelain, and silver, Ole Kortzau (born 1939) has maintained his own design firm since 1972. He has had several solo exhibitions and is currently working with the Royal Copenhagen Porcelain Manufactory. He has designed silver holloware for the Georg Jensen Silversmithy since 1978.

98. *Bowls [1244, 1246]*
     designs introduced 1979
     hand-chased and sculpted
     sterling silver
     height x width x depth:
     34 x 195 x 145 mm, lower left;
     27 x 155 x 145 mm, upper right
     145 mm, upper right

99. *Vase [1248]*
     design introduced 1979
     hand-chased and sculpted
     sterling silver
     height: 152 mm

ANETTE KRÆN

Anette Kræn (born 1945) attended the Danish College of Jewelry, Silversmithing, and Commercial Design from 1967 to 1969 and studied in Germany and Switzerland until 1974. She has been represented in several exhibitions in Denmark and elsewhere and has won awards at competitions held by the Association of Danish Goldsmiths. She has been employed as a designer by the Georg Jensen Silversmithy since 1978.

100. *Necklace* [310]
     design introduced 1979
     cast and chased sterling silver,
     mounted on leather with hand-
     made clasp
     length: 432 mm

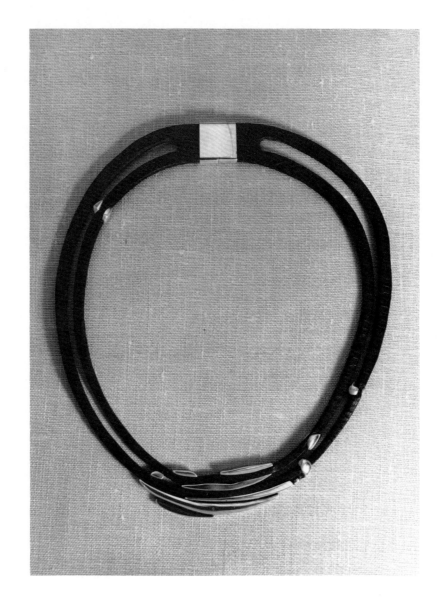

HUGO LIISBERG

The sculptor Hugo Liisberg (1896-1958) completed his apprenticeship at the Royal Copenhagen Porcelain Manufactory in 1915. He was awarded a gold medal by the Royal Danish Academy of Fine Arts and the Eckersberg Medal in 1942.

101. *Brooch [299]*
     design introduced 1943
     cast and chased sterling silver
     diameter: 53 mm

ERIK MAGNUSSEN

Erik Magnussen (born 1940) graduated in 1960 from the Danish School of Arts, Crafts, and Design in Copenhagen. He maintains his own workshop and designs stoneware, glass, cutlery, and furniture. He also works with the Bing & Grøndahl Porcelain Manufactory. Among his awards are a silver medal received in 1960 from the Technical Association of Prize Subjects (Det Tekniske Selskabs Prisopgaver) and the Lunning Prize received in 1967. His work is represented in the collections of several museums, including the Victoria and Albert Museum in London. Magnussen has designed silver holloware for the Georg Jensen Silversmithy since 1978.

102. *Thermos Pitcher [1238]*
design introduced 1978
soldered sterling silver tube with cast handle and thermoplastic top
height: 298 mm

ARNO MALINOWSKI

A sculptor and engraver, Arno Malinowski (1899-1976) was educated at the Royal Danish Academy of Fine Arts. He executed many figurines for the Royal Copenhagen Porcelain Manufactory and worked with the Georg Jensen Silversmithy from 1936 to 1965. He received a silver medal at the Paris World Exhibition in 1925 and the Eckersberg Medal in 1933. Among Malinowski's productions for the Jensen company was the Kongemærket, an emblem in silver and enamel that he designed on the occasion of the seventieth birthday of His Majesty Christian X and which was worn by thousands of Danes during World War II as a symbol of their patriotism.

103. *Tie Clip* [83]
Not illustrated
design introduced 1964
cast sterling silver
length: 42 mm

104. *Medal*
design introduced 1959
sterling silver
diameter: 42 mm

105. *Brooch* [256]
design introduced 1942
pressed and hand-carved sterling
silver
diameter: 45 mm

106. *Brooch* [284]
design introduced 1942; deleted
from production 1962
pressed and handcut sterling
silver with enameled leaves
diameter: 33 mm

ANDREAS MIKKELSEN

Associated with the Jensen
silverworks for many years,
Andreas Mikkelsen (born 1928) is
currently the director of sales,
production, and product development for the Georg Jensen
Silversmithy.

107. *Armring [A76G]*
design introduced 1973
hand-forged sterling silver with
handmade hinge and clasp
diameter: 81 mm

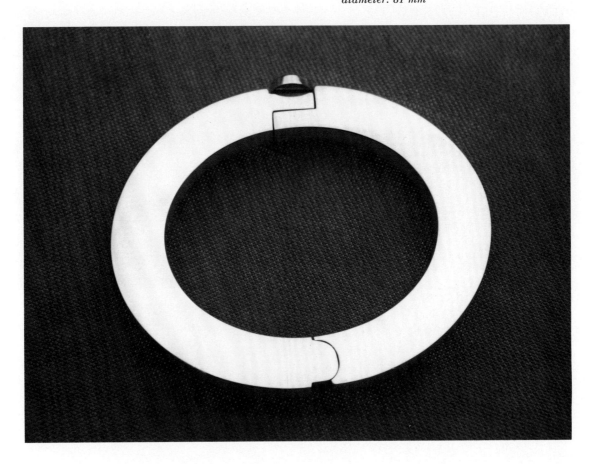

108. *Money Clip* [*A1003*]
     design introduced 1973
     hand-formed 14k gold wire
     diameter: 45 mm

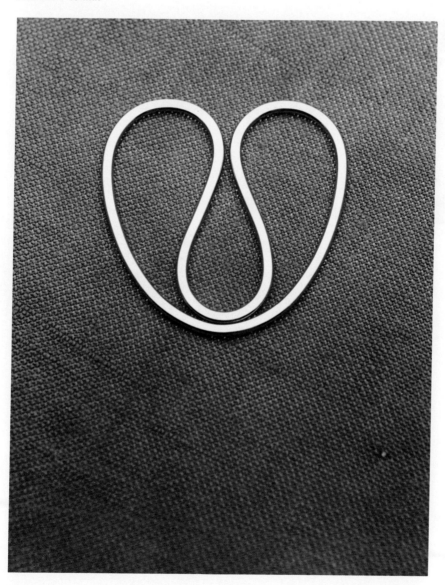

KRISTIAN
MØHL-HANSEN

Kristian Møhl-Hansen (1876-1962) studied painting at the Royal Danish Academy of Fine Arts and the Zahrtmann School. He was given several scholarships and grants allowing him to travel to Germany, France, Italy, England, Spain, and Holland. He was awarded the Eckersberg Medal in 1920 and a gold medal for his embroidered textiles at the Paris World Exhibition in 1925.

109. *Cup [203]*
     design introduced 1916; deleted from production 1930
     hand-raised and chased sterling silver, mounted with amber
     height x diameter: 66 x 100 mm

KIM NAVER

A weaver who has maintained her own workshop since 1966, Kim Naver (born 1940) designs industrial and ecclesiastical textiles and makes unique tapestries and carpets. Her awards and grants include the Lunning Prize received in 1970. She has designed jewelry for the Georg Jensen Silversmithy since 1971.

110. *Miniature Pendants* [972, 982, 983, 989]
      designs introduced 1978
      cast 18k gold
      diameter: 7 to 10 mm, range

111. *Armring* [253]
      design introduced 1973
      cast and chased sterling silver
      diameter: 68 mm

HARALD NIELSEN

Harald Nielsen (1892-1977)
joined the Georg Jensen Silversmithy in 1909 and was Georg
Jensen's closest colleague. He
served the Jensen company as a
silver designer and artistic director for nearly thirty years.
Nielsen designed the Jensen
series of double-fluted tableware.

112. *Bread Tray* [761]
   design introduced 1937
   hand-chased sterling silver
   height x width x depth:
   85 x 245 x 145 mm

113. *Candlestick* [604C]
      Illustrated on page 16
      design introduced 1930
      hand-forged, sculpted, and
      chased sterling silver
      height: 100 mm

114. *Bracelet* [86]
      design introduced 1945
      sterling silver links, individually
      pressed and hinged together
      length: 178 mm

115. *Ring* [46E]
      design introduced 1957
      cast and handmade sterling
      silver frames, mounted with
      hematite
      diameter: 34 mm

116. *Ring* [76]
      design introduced 1935
      cast and handmade sterling
      silver frames, mounted with
      lapis lazuli
      diameter: 10 mm

GUSTAV PEDERSEN

Gustav Pedersen (1895-1972)
began working at the Georg
Jensen Silversmithy in 1915 and
was appointed foreman of the
holloware department in 1917.
He retired from the company in
1965.

117. *Gravy Boat* [766]
*design introduced 1938; deleted
from production 1960
hand-raised and engraved
sterling silver with ebony
diameter: 195 mm*

ARNE PETERSEN

Arne Petersen (born 1922) joined
the Georg Jensen Silversmithy
in 1948. Since 1976 he has been
employed in the Jensen holloware
department.

118. *Bottle Opener* [7008]
      design introduced 1975
      pressed stainless steel and brass,
      soldered together
      diameter: 63 mm

BENT HOLSE PETERSEN   Bent Holse Petersen (born 1928) has been employed in the gold-smith workshop of the Georg Jensen Silversmithy since 1952.

119.   *Cuff Links [114]*
design introduced 1966
pressed sterling silver buttons
with handmade links
width: 22 mm

120.   *Cuff Links [115]*
design introduced 1966
pressed sterling silver buttons
with handmade links
width: 22 mm

OLE BENT PETERSEN

During the late 1950s Ole Bent Petersen (born 1938) studied at the Danish College of Jewelry, Silversmithing, and Commercial Design and the Royal Danish Academy of Fine Arts. He has maintained his own workshop since 1960 and has been affiliated with the Georg Jensen Silversmithy since 1978.

121. *Sculpture* [1]
     design introduced 1979
     18k and 24k gold sheets and wire, soldered together with ivory base
     height: 115 mm

HENRY PILSTRUP

Georg Jensen's first apprentice,
Henry Pilstrup (1890-1967),
joined the silversmithy in 1904.
While foreman of the jewelry
workshop from 1918 to 1957, he
designed various pieces of gold
and silver jewelry.

122. *Cuff Links* [64]
design introduced 1937
pressed sterling silver buttons
with handmade links
width: 24 mm

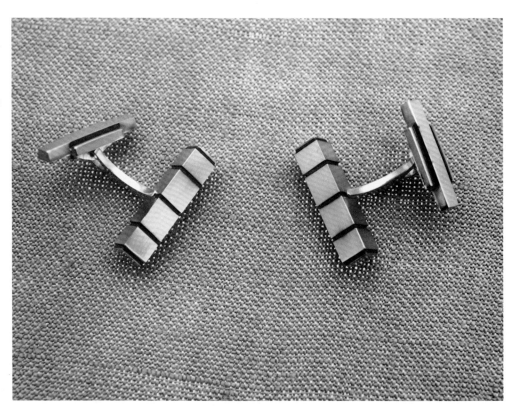

JOHAN ROHDE

As a young man Johan Rohde (1856-1935) studied medicine, but he took an interest in art and entered the Royal Danish Academy of Fine Arts in 1882. In that same year he founded the Artists' Studio School for which he taught anatomy. His paintings were exhibited at the academy for the first time in 1888. In 1903 Rohde began his professional association with Georg Jensen by commissioning him to fabricate objects that Rohde had designed for his personal use. Rohde and Jensen gradually formed a closer bond and Rohde created many designs that are still in production today. One of the most famous is the Acorn pattern, which has been the company's best selling cutlery pattern. Rohde also designed textiles and furniture.

123. *Clock* [333]
    Illustrated on page 16
    design introduced 1919
    bent, chased, and shaped
    sterling silver
    height: 280 mm

124. *Tea Pot* [787]
    design introduced 1933-36
    spun and hand-raised sterling
    silver with ebony
    diameter: 155 mm

JOHAN ROHDE

125. *Plate* [587]
design introduced 1930
chased and spun sterling silver
diameter: 280 mm

126. *Candlestick* [286]
design introduced 1919
raised, shaped, and hammered
sterling silver base with stem
made of three hollow parts,
soldered together
height: 228 mm

127. *Sugar Caster* [276]
     design introduced 1918; deleted
     from production 1938
     raised, chased, shaped, drilled,
     and engraved sterling silver
     height: 100 mm

128. *Box for Cards and Chips* [478]
     design introduced 1926
     raised, bent, and chased
     sterling silver
     height: 170 mm

JOHAN ROHDE

129. *Soup Ladle*
      design introduced 1906
      raised and hammered sterling
      silver with sculpted handle
      length: 290 mm

130. *Cutlery, Acorn Pattern* [62]
      Illustrated on page 14 and with
      number 125
      design introduced 1915
      sterling silver with stainless
      steel blades
      salad fork length: 165 mm
      fork length: 190 mm
      knife length: 230 mm
      soup spoon length: 160 mm
      teaspoon length: 155 mm
      butter knife length: 150 mm

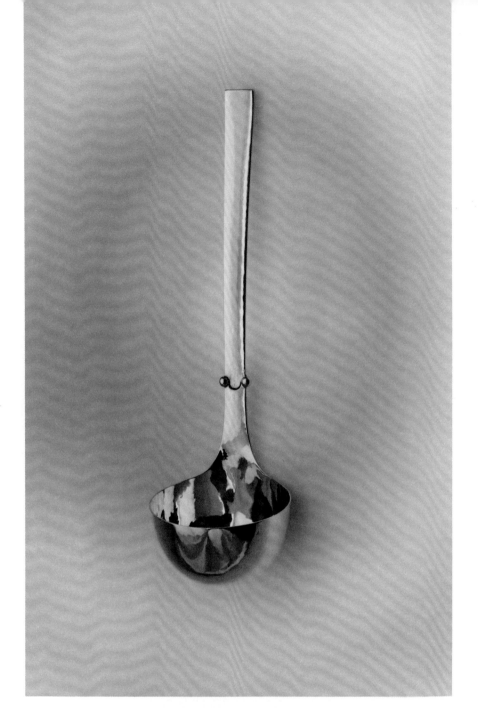

ANTON ROSEN

An architect and designer, Anton Rosen (1858-1928) designed the Palace Hotel in Copenhagen. He also was the principal architect for the National Exhibition (Landsudstillingen) held at Århus, Denmark, in 1909.

131. *Cup of the Butchers' Guild*
      [*unique object, not exhibited*]
      designed 1917
      hand-sculpted sterling silver
      height: 1150 mm

STEPHAN ROSTRUP

A sculptor and painter, Stephan
Rostrup (born 1947) has
designed silver sculptures and
jewelry for the Georg Jensen
Silversmithy since 1978.

132. *Sculpture [1253]*
design introduced 1979
cast and chased sterling silver
height: 135 mm

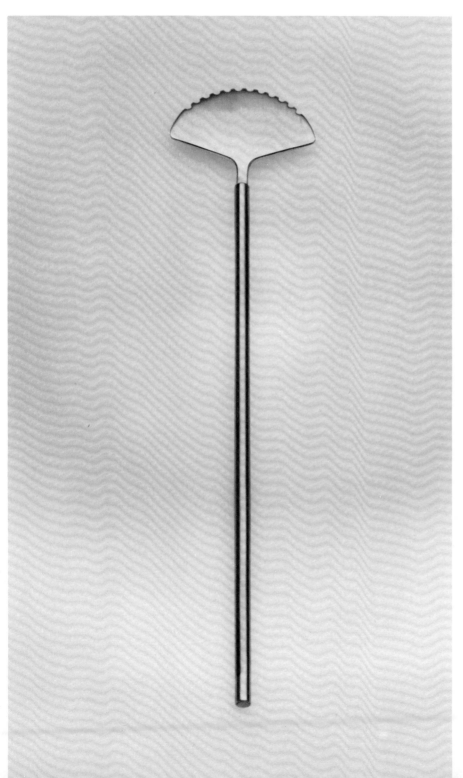

GEORG SCHÜTT

Educated as a goldsmith at the workshop of A. Michelsen, Georg Schütt (born 1928) furthered his education in Stockholm before starting work in the design department of the Georg Jensen Silversmithy in 1951. He became the manager of the company's advertising department and is now public relations officer for the Association of Danish Furniture Manufacturers.

133.   *Mixing Strainer [400]*
       design introduced 1958
       forged stainless steel
       length: 310 mm

HENNING SEIDELIN

A sculptor and designer of silver, steel, porcelain, and faïence, Henning Seidelin (born 1904) is represented in several Danish museums. He was awarded the Eckersberg Medal in 1951 and gold medals at the Milan Triennale in 1951 and 1954.

134. *Candlestick* [668A]
       design introduced 1932
       spun and soldered sterling silver
       height: 39 mm

THOR SELZER

Trained as a goldsmith, Thor
Selzer (born 1925) has maintained his own workshop since
1957. His work is in the collections of many museums,
including the Danish Museum of
Decorative Art in Copenhagen.

135. *Armring* [236]
     design introduced 1972
     cast and open sterling silver
     diameter: 66 mm

136. *Rings* [164]
     design introduced 1972
     cast and open sterling silver
     diameter: 13 mm, each

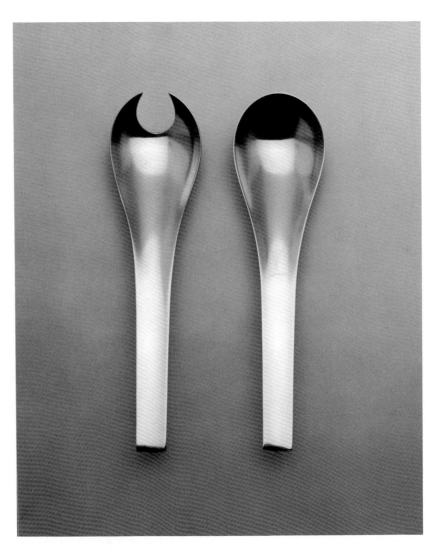

SVEND SIUNE

Svend Siune (born 1935) graduated in 1961 from the School of Arts, Crafts, and Design in Copenhagen and has since then designed furniture and cutlery.

137. *Serving Fork and Spoon, Blue Shark Pattern* [325]
design introduced 1965
forged and hand-polished stainless steel
length: 205 mm, each

EVA STÆHR-NIELSEN

A ceramics designer and the
wife of sculptor Olaf Stæhr-
Nielsen, Eva Stæhr-Nielsen
(1911-1967) was associated first
with Saxbo and later with the
Royal Copenhagen Porcelain
Manufactory.

138. *Mocha Spoons* [112]
      design introduced 1958
      forged and hand-enameled
      sterling silver
      length: 100 mm, each

OLAF STÆHR-NIELSEN

Olaf Stæhr-Nielsen (1896-1969)
was a sculptor who also designed
ceramics, silver, and furniture.

139. Bracelet [806]
      design introduced 1961
      bent and soldered 18k gold wire
      with turquoise
      length: 178 mm

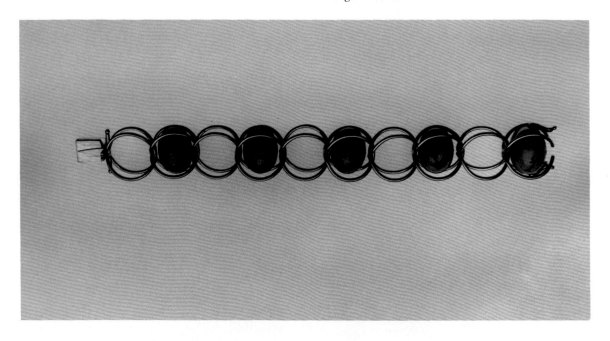

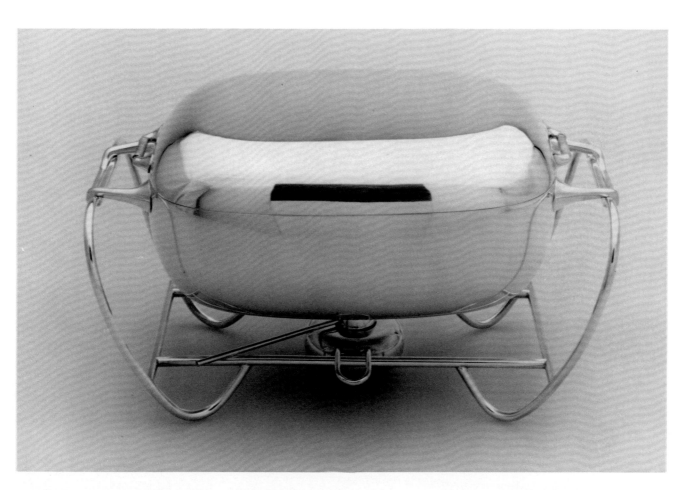

MAGNUS STEPHENSEN

An architect and designer, Magnus Stephensen (born 1903) completed his technical schooling in 1924. He studied at the Royal Danish Academy of Fine Arts until 1930 and the French School in Athens in 1931. He has designed award-winning apartment buildings, rowhouses, schools, and waterworks. His architectural renderings and silver and stainless steel designs are included in the collections of many European and American museums. His awards include the Eckersberg Medal received in 1948 and several medals

received at the Milan Triennale: gold medals in 1951 and 1957, the Grand Prix in 1954, and a silver medal in 1960. Stephensen has been associated with the Georg Jensen Silversmithy since 1950 and has designed holloware and such sterling silver and stainless steel cutlery patterns as Tanaquil and Frigate.

140. *Chafing Dish* [1055]
design introduced 1956
raised and hammered
sterling silver
height x width: 290 x 170 mm

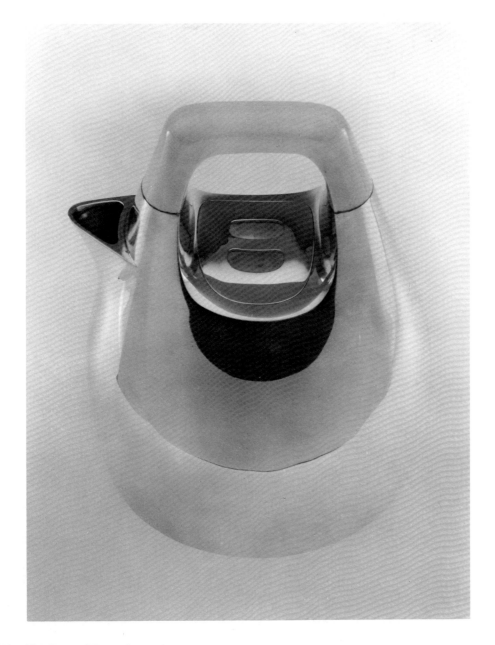

141. *Tea Pot and Water Jug* [39]
      design introduced 1957; deleted
      from production circa 1970
      forged stainless steel
      height: 185 mm

142. *Tea Pot* [1022]
      design introduced 1953
      sterling silver with ivory
      diameter: 148 mm

SIEGFRIED WAGNER

Siegfried Wagner (1874-1952)
was a sculptor whose work
The Lure Players, 1914, was
placed in Town Hall Square in
Copenhagen.

143. *Cutlery, Dahlia Pattern* [3]
    design introduced 1912
    forged and hand-polished
    sterling silver
    fork length: 183 mm
    knife length: 220 mm
    spoon length: 180 mm

OLE WANSCHER

An architect, designer, and author, Ole Wanscher (born 1903) designs furniture based on eighteenth-century English models. From 1953 until 1973 he was professor of architecture at the Royal Danish Academy of Fine Arts.

144. *Competition Proposal*
       design proposed 1966
       sterling silver
       spoon length: 195 mm
       fork length: 195 mm
       teaspoon length: 112 mm

OVE WENDT Trained as a silversmith, Ove Wendt (born 1907) has maintained his own workshop since 1959. He worked with Andreas Mikkelsen from 1970 to 1978 and has designed jewelry for the Jensen silverworks since 1978.

145. *Armring [A12]*
Not illustrated
design introduced 1948
raised and sculpted sterling silver
diameter: 65 mm

146. *Neckring [A23A]*
design introduced 1948
raised and sculpted sterling silver
diameter: 140 mm

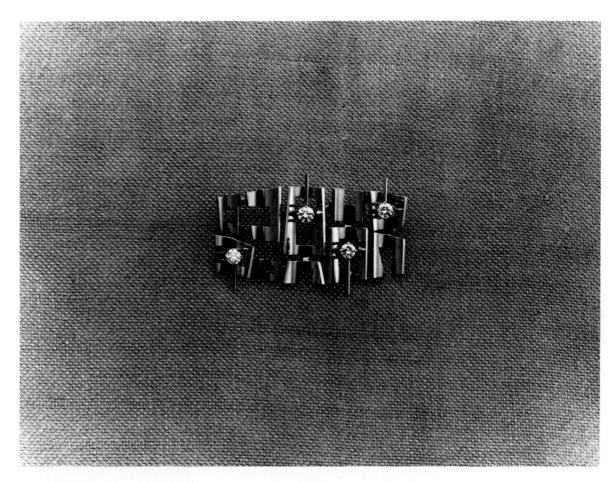

OTHMAR ZSCHALER

A native of Switzerland, where
he maintains his own workshop,
Othmar Zschaler (born 1930) is
a goldsmith whose jewelry is represented in many European
museums.

147. *Brooch* [835]
      design introduced 1961
      cut and soldered 18k gold sheet
      with diamonds
      length: 45 mm

COMPANY MARKS

A catalogue of all marks
used by the Georg Jensen
Silversmithy is not complete. The
following information was
compiled by Georg Jensen Sølvsmedie
A/S, Copenhagen, in
August 1978.

1904-1908
Used together

1909-1914
Used together

1915-1927
Embossed on base

1915-1930

1925-1932

1933-1944

GEORGJENSEN
& WENDEL A/S

1945-1951
Used exclusively for goods sold
through the sales shop Georg
Jensen & Wendel A/S, Copenhagen

Since 1945
Used on jewelry, cutlery, and
holloware, but not on objects
made of stainless steel or other
nonprecious metals.

Since 1945
Used only on small items such as
charms.

SELECTED BIBLIOGRAPHY

Entries are arranged chronologically.

Nielsen, L. C. *Georg Jensen.* Copenhagen: Fr. Bagge Printers, 1921.

Georg Jensen. Paris: Editions des Quatre Chemins [1925].

Nielsen, Laurits Christian. *En Dansk kunstner virksomhed; Georg Jensen sølvet gennem 25 aar* [A Danish art manufacturer; Georg Jensen silver through 25 years]. Copenhagen: C. C. Petersen, 1929.

Olsen, Ivan Munk. *Sølvsmeden Georg Jensen* [The Silversmith Georg Jensen]. Dansk Kunst [Danish Art], vol. 4. Text in Danish and English. Copenhagen: Arthur Jensens, 1937.

"Georg Jensen Solv" [Georg Jensen silver]. *Samleren* [The collector]. Special Edition, 2 (1938).

Reventlow, Christian Ditlev. *Georg Jensen sølvsmedie gennem fyrretyve aar, 1904-1944* [Georg Jensen's silversmithy through forty years]. Copenhagen: Nordlund [1944].

Weilbach, Philip. *Kunstnerleksikon* [Art dictionary], vol. 1. Copenhagen: Aschehoug, 1947.

Schultz, Sigurd. *Johan Rohde Sølv* [Johan Rohde silver]. Copenhagen: Fischers, 1951.

Stovenow, Åke, and Reventlow, Christian Ditlev. *Harald Nielsen, Et tilbageblik på en kunstners arbejder ved 60-arsdagen* [Harald Nielsen, a retrospective of an artist's work on his 60th birthday]. Copenhagen: Georg Jensen & Wendel, Inc., 1952.

Hiort, Esbjørn. *Modern Danish Silver.* New York: Museum Books; London: Zwemmer, 1954.

Fifty Years of Danish Silver in the Georg Jensen Tradition. Copenhagen: Schønberg, 1954; New York [1955].

Johansson, Gotthard, and Reventlow, Christian Ditlev. *Sigvard Bernadotte Sølvarbejder, 1930-1955* [Sigvard Bernadotte silverwork]. Copenhagen: Georg Jensen Sølv, 1955.

Schwartz, Walter. *Georg Jensen, en kunstner, hans tid og slaegt* [Georg Jensen, an artist, his time and heritage]. Copenhagen: Georg Jensen & Wendel, Inc., 1958.

The Arts of Denmark, Viking to Modern. Copenhagen: Det Berlingske Bogtrykkeri, 1960.

Hughes, Graham. *Modern Jewelry, An International Survey, 1890-1963.* London: Studio Books; New York: Crown Publishers, Inc., 1963.

Møller, Viggo Sten. *Henning Koppel.* Translated into English by Ellen Branth, into German by Albrecht Leonhardt. Copenhagen: Rhodos, 1965.

Hughes, Graham. *Modern Silver throughout the World, 1880-1967.* London: Studio Vista Limited; New York: Crown Publishers, Inc., 1967.

Møller, Viggo Sten. *Dansk Kunstindustri, 1850-1900* [Danish art industry]. Copenhagen: Rhodos, 1969.

Hughes, Graham. *The Art of Jewelry.* New York: Viking Press; London: Studio Vista Limited, 1972.

Møller, Henrik Sten. *Dansk Design* [Danish design]. Translated into English by Douglas Holmes. Copenhagen: Rhodos, 1975.

Dansk Kunsthåndvaerker Leksikon [Danish craftsman dictionary]. Copenhagen: Rhodos, 1979.

This book was produced by the Smithsonian Institution Press, Washington, D. C.
Composed by General Typographers, Inc., Washington, D. C.,
in Bodoni Book with display heads in Engravers Bold.
Printed by Eastern Press, Inc., New Haven, Connecticut,
on eighty-pound Mead Black-and-White Gloss with Color Text endpapers.
Case edition bound by Riverside Binding, Rochester, New York,
in Holliston B-grade Roxite, linen finish,
and stamped in silver.
Paperback edition bound by Riverside Binding, Rochester, New York, in Mead Cover.
Designed by Stephen Kraft.

Library of Congress Cataloging in Publication Data

Main entry under title:
Georg Jensen Silversmithy.
  "Published on the occasion of an exhibition
organized by and held at the Renwick Gallery of the
National Collection of Fine Arts, Smithsonian Institution,
Washington, D. C., February 29 — July 6, 1980."
  Bibliography: p.
  1. Georg Jensen sølvsmedie, A/s — Exhibitions.
2. Silverwork — Denmark — History — 20th century —
Exhibitions. I. Renwick Gallery.
NK7198.G38A4 1980   739.2' 3722   79-607160
ISBN 0-87474-800-3
ISBN 0-87474-801-1 pbk.